Learning Firefox OS Application Development

Learn to design, build, and deploy your Firefox
OS applications, built with web technologies,
to the Firefox Marketplace

Tanay Pant

[PACKT] open source*
PUBLISHING   community experience distilled

BIRMINGHAM - MUMBAI

Learning Firefox OS Application Development

First published: October 2015

Production reference: 1061015

Published by Packt Publishing Ltd.
Livery Place
35 Livery Street
Birmingham B3 2PB, UK.

ISBN 978-1-78398-940-9

www.packtpub.com

Credits

Author
Tanay Pant

Reviewers
Dietrich Ayala
Kumar Rishav

Commissioning Editor
Ashwin Nair

Acquisition Editor
Manish Nainani

Content Development Editor
Merwyn D'souza

Technical Editor
Utkarsha S. Kadam

Copy Editors
Imon Biswas
Vikrant Phadke

Project Coordinator
Neha Bhatnagar

Proofreader
Safis Editing

Indexer
Rekha Nair

Production Coordinator
Aparna Bhagat

Cover Work
Aparna Bhagat

Foreword

Mozilla is a global community of technologists, thinkers, and builders working together to keep the Internet alive and accessible so that people worldwide can be informed contributors and creators of the Web. Our mission is to promote openness, innovation, and opportunities on the Web.

Firefox OS is our latest effort to put open and decentralized technologies of the Web at the heart of where the Internet goes next—beyond desktops and even smartphones—to encompass what some call the "Internet of Things," namely smart objects that talk to each other and to you. At Mozilla, we aspire to show you that all connected devices can be as open as the Web on our desktops, and ultimately help build a world where all our devices—and all of the data we create that connects them—give us choice, independence, and agency.

As a Mozilla rep, Tanay Pant has done a stellar job to help push the Mozilla mission forward across India and beyond, with a particular focus on helping talented developers learn how to contribute code to our various projects, including Firefox OS.

Learning Firefox OS Application Development is an excellent introduction to the Firefox OS project and shows you how to contribute to it from an application development perspective. I hope this book becomes a great resource for you and encourages you to become not only an active contributor to the Firefox OS platform, but also a strong advocate of our mission. Thank you for your interest in Mozilla and in helping us keep the Web open and participative. Happy reading!

May the source be with you!

William Quiviger

Global Community Manager, Mozilla

About the Author

Tanay Pant is a developer, white hat, and writer who has a passion for web development. He contributes code to Mozilla Webmaker and is the chief architect of Stock Wolf (`www.stockwolf.net`), a global virtual stock trading platform that aims to impart practical education about stocks and markets. He is also a representative of Mozilla, and you can find his name listed under the credits (`https://www.mozilla.org/credits/`) of the Firefox web browser. You can also find articles written by him on web development at SitePoint and TutsPlus. Tanay acts as a security consultant and enjoys helping corporations fix vulnerabilities in their products.

I would like to express my gratitude to my father for being such a wonderful inspiration in my life, and my mother for being the most supportive person that I have ever seen.

I would like to thank my family, professors at the university, friends at Mozilla and Packt Publishing, and the many people who helped me through this book.

Then, I would like to thank Shubham Oli, who helped me to write chapters 6 and 7 and also to develop the various applications that have been included in this book.

I would also like to mention the names of my professors—Dr. H.L. Mandoria, Sanjay Joshi, Rajesh Shyam Singh, B.K. Pandey, Ashok Kumar, and S.P. Dwivedi of the College of Technology, Pantnagar—who encouraged and supported me in writing this book.

My deepest gratitude to all the teachers who have taught me from kindergarten to engineering.

About the Reviewers

Dietrich Ayala is a technical evangelist at Mozilla. He has been building web software designed to preserve choice and innovation on the Internet for nearly a decade, including the Firefox browser, the Firefox OS, and a number of other Mozilla projects. Before Mozilla, he spent time at Yahoo!, McAfee, Sub Pop Records, and various start-ups. He resides in Portland, Oregon, USA.

Kumar Rishav has been contributing to the Firefox OS project for the past 2 years. He is an open source enthusiast and evangelist. He was an intern at the Google Summer of Code 2014. Kumar is an application developer, coding freak, and bug hunter.

> I would like to thank Tanay Pant for coming up with such awesome content. It is written in a nice way. Also, thanks to my mentors, Julien, Oleg, and Gabriele (Mozilla Employees), for always guiding me and showing me the right direction to work in.

www.PacktPub.com

Support files, eBooks, discount offers, and more

For support files and downloads related to your book, please visit www.PacktPub.com.

Did you know that Packt offers eBook versions of every book published, with PDF and ePub files available? You can upgrade to the eBook version at www.PacktPub.com and as a print book customer, you are entitled to a discount on the eBook copy. Get in touch with us at service@packtpub.com for more details.

At www.PacktPub.com, you can also read a collection of free technical articles, sign up for a range of free newsletters and receive exclusive discounts and offers on Packt books and eBooks.

https://www2.packtpub.com/books/subscription/packtlib

Do you need instant solutions to your IT questions? PacktLib is Packt's online digital book library. Here, you can search, access, and read Packt's entire library of books.

Why subscribe?

- Fully searchable across every book published by Packt
- Copy and paste, print, and bookmark content
- On demand and accessible via a web browser

Free access for Packt account holders

If you have an account with Packt at www.PacktPub.com, you can use this to access PacktLib today and view 9 entirely free books. Simply use your login credentials for immediate access.

Table of Contents

Preface

Mozilla publicly demonstrated the open source Firefox OS in February 2012. Firefox OS is an initiative by the open source company Mozilla to develop a mobile platform for smartphones as well as a host of other devices, such as tablets and televisions. The reason for rolling out this platform was to provide its users with an operating system that has an alternative that respects the user's privacy and puts security first. Firefox OS devices are a great choice for users who are transitioning from feature phones to smartphones or those who are concerned about privacy. Mozilla is best known for developing pieces of open source software, such as the Firefox web browser, and it doesn't answer its users rather than answering to stakeholders. The aim of Firefox OS is to run on devices that have limited hardware capabilities while still providing a unique and smooth user experience.

Mozilla has a huge community of developers and users, and they are always willing to help others on platforms such as GitHub and IRC (irc.mozilla.org). Firefox OS also has a great marketplace. It has grown over the years and offers great applications. In Firefox OS, HTML5 applications are first-class applications, and so any ordinary web application can be turned into a Firefox OS application in just a few steps. Even the user interface of Firefox OS, which is known as Gecko, has been built with the help of three components, namely HTML5, JavaScript, and CSS3. This makes developing applications easy for people who have already done web development.

What this book covers

Chapter 1, Introduction to Firefox OS, improves your understanding of Firefox OS by teaching its terminology, abstraction layer, and security model.

Chapter 2, Running Firefox OS Simulators with WebIDE, teaches you how to use WebIDE; install, uninstall, and create new applications; and use developer tools for applications running in WebIDE.

Chapter 3, Getting Your Hands Dirty – Firefox OS Apps, introduces the difference between packaged and hosted applications, security access levels of different Firefox OS applications, and developing application manifest files for apps.

Chapter 4, Diving Deeper with the Fox Creating Richer Apps, teaches you how to make hosted Firefox OS applications installable and offline. It then shows you how to apply web APIs to applications.

Chapter 5, Making Applications Visually Appealing – A Style Guide, takes you through the basic designing guidelines. These will help you make applications more user friendly. This chapter also tells you how to avoid some common UI blunders and apply the Gaia building blocks.

Chapter 6, Emerging as a Guru – Learning Web APIs, teaches web APIs, types of web APIs, web activities, and how to use them. This chapter also teaches you to implement all your acquired knowledge to build FoxFoto, a photo editing and sharing application.

Chapter 7, Testing Your Firefox OS Application, covers basic QA and unit testing, using Firefox developer tools for debugging, using the app validator to test applications, and using a spoof Firefox add-on for testing to improve the performance of a Firefox OS application.

Chapter 8, Firefox Marketplace – Setting up Your Bazaar, takes you through the Firefox Marketplace and shows you how to submit and update free and paid applications in the marketplace.

Chapter 9, Maintaining Your Firefox OS Application Code Professionally, takes you through setting up an account on GitHub, version controlling your Firefox OS application, and uploading the local repository to GitHub. It also teaches you how to set up Travis CI for your repository and host applications on RHCloud with the help of Git.

What you need for this book

You will need the following:

- The latest version of Firefox available
- Firefox OS Simulator (2.0)
- An Android device running the Firefox web browser (optional)
- A device running Firefox OS 2.0 (optional)

Who this book is for

This is a practical guide that uses hands-on examples to teach you how to create applications for Firefox OS and also how to port applications to the Firefox Marketplace. This book is intended for developers who want to build applications for Firefox OS. An understanding of HTML5, JavaScript, and CSS is required.

Conventions

In this book, you will find a number of text styles that distinguish between different kinds of information. Here are some examples of these styles and an explanation of their meaning.

Code words in text, database table names, folder names, filenames, file extensions, pathnames, dummy URLs, user input, and Twitter handles are shown as follows: "I have replaced World with Firefox everywhere to make it Hello Firefox."

A block of code is set as follows:

```
<script src="js/jquery-1.11.3.min.js"></script>
<script src="js/bootstrap.min.js"></script>
<script src="js/clickr.js"></script>
```

New terms and **important words** are shown in bold. Words that you see on the screen, for example, in menus or dialog boxes, appear in the text like this: "When you click on it, you will see the **Install Simulator** option."

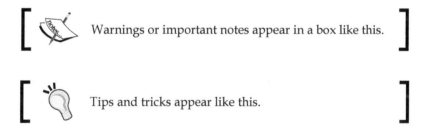

Warnings or important notes appear in a box like this.

Tips and tricks appear like this.

Reader feedback

Feedback from our readers is always welcome. Let us know what you think about this book—what you liked or disliked. Reader feedback is important for us as it helps us develop titles that you will really get the most out of.

To send us general feedback, simply e-mail feedback@packtpub.com, and mention the book's title in the subject of your message.

If there is a topic that you have expertise in and you are interested in either writing or contributing to a book, see our author guide at www.packtpub.com/authors.

Customer support

Now that you are the proud owner of a Packt book, we have a number of things to help you to get the most from your purchase.

Downloading the example code

You can download the example code files from your account at http://www.packtpub.com for all the Packt Publishing books you have purchased. If you purchased this book elsewhere, you can visit http://www.packtpub.com/support and register to have the files e-mailed directly to you.

Downloading the color images of this book

We also provide you with a PDF file that has color images of the screenshots/diagrams used in this book. The color images will help you better understand the changes in the output. You can download this file from https://www.packtpub.com/sites/default/files/downloads/9409OS.pdf.

Errata

Although we have taken every care to ensure the accuracy of our content, mistakes do happen. If you find a mistake in one of our books—maybe a mistake in the text or the code—we would be grateful if you could report this to us. By doing so, you can save other readers from frustration and help us improve subsequent versions of this book. If you find any errata, please report them by visiting http://www.packtpub.com/submit-errata, selecting your book, clicking on the **Errata Submission Form** link, and entering the details of your errata. Once your errata are verified, your submission will be accepted and the errata will be uploaded to our website or added to any list of existing errata under the Errata section of that title.

To view the previously submitted errata, go to https://www.packtpub.com/books/content/support and enter the name of the book in the search field. The required information will appear under the **Errata** section.

Piracy

Piracy of copyrighted material on the Internet is an ongoing problem across all media. At Packt, we take the protection of our copyright and licenses very seriously. If you come across any illegal copies of our works in any form on the Internet, please provide us with the location address or website name immediately so that we can pursue a remedy.

Please contact us at copyright@packtpub.com with a link to the suspected pirated material.

We appreciate your help in protecting our authors and our ability to bring you valuable content.

Questions

If you have a problem with any aspect of this book, you can contact us at questions@packtpub.com, and we will do our best to address the problem.

1

Introduction to Firefox OS

In this chapter, you will improve your understanding of Firefox OS by learning about its terminology, architecture, abstraction layers, as well as the security model. We will discuss the reasons why it makes sense to develop or port applications to Firefox OS. We will also take a look at the Firefox OS devices currently available in the global market. We will go through the following topics in detail:

- Getting to know about Firefox OS
- Why you should develop applications for Firefox OS
- Technical details of Firefox OS
- The security model of the OS
- Devices on the market that run Firefox OS

Introducing Firefox OS

Mozilla and Telefónica started a joint project in 2011 under the code name Boot to Gecko—a new mobile operating system built on top of a web technology. Mozilla publicly demonstrated the open source Firefox OS in February 2012. The reason to roll out this platform was to provide developers with an alternative operating system that respects the user's privacy and security so that new smartphone users have a choice in buying. Firefox OS devices are a great choice for users who wish to make a transition from feature phones to smartphones, or for those who have concerns about the privacy settings. Mozilla is best known for developing open source software, such as Firefox Web Browser, and it answers to its users rather than answering to its stakeholders. The aim of Firefox OS is to run on devices that have limited hardware capabilities while still providing users with a unique and smooth experience.

Let's now take a look at a screenshot of a device that uses Firefox OS:

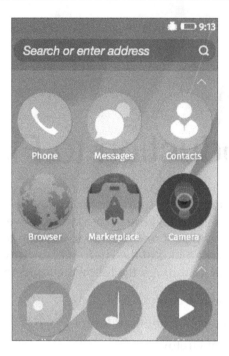

The need to develop applications for Firefox OS

Firefox OS is one of the emerging platforms in the market, with devices having been released in a large number of countries. Developing applications for Firefox OS is very easy, especially for web developers, as Firefox OS treats HTML5 applications as first-class citizens, and hence there isn't any requirement to learn about using any unique platform-specific **SDK**.

The greatest thing about developing applications for Firefox OS is that the apps that you construct can run on a host of other devices that run Firefox as well, the goal being to make the Firefox OS apps to run in any web browser. For example, if the application that you build is responsive, then you will also be able to install and run it on a computer/laptop that runs Firefox. Isn't that great? Firefox is available for Windows, OS X, Linux, and Android, and very soon it will be available for iOS as well! This will allow you to distribute your applications to a wide number of people using different platforms. Also, unlike platforms such as iOS, you are not forced to publish your applications via the official marketplace; you can host your applications by yourself as well.

Mozilla has a huge community of developers and users, who are always willing to help others on platforms such as GitHub and IRC (`https://wiki.mozilla.org/IRC`). Firefox OS also has a great marketplace, which has grown over the years and offers great applications. Even the user interface of Firefox OS, which is known as Gaia, is built with the help of three components, namely HTML5, JavaScript, and CSS3. This makes developing applications for this platform easy for people who have experience in web development.

You can also port the applications that you build for Firefox OS to native applications for other platforms with the use of software such as PhoneGap, since Firefox OS applications are essentially web applications.

The architecture of Firefox OS

The architecture of Firefox OS is a bit different from other mobile operating systems. There are three levels of abstraction in Firefox OS: Gonk, Gecko, and Gaia.

Mobile hardware

Mobile hardware refers to the various components present in a mobile, such as the battery, sensors, camera, GPS, Bluetooth, and other things, that are crucial for the interaction of the operating system with the device and environment. The interaction of these various components with the operating system is what makes the experience of smartphones unique compared to the previous generation of phones, called feature phones.

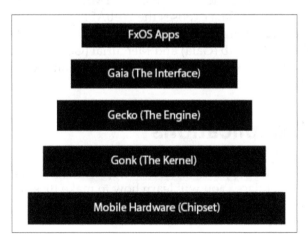

Gonk – the kernel

Firefox OS's kernel is built in the Android Open Source Project, which itself is a Linux kernel, and is the lowest level in the abstraction structure of the operating system. Gonk acts as the interface between the underlying hardware and Gecko. It deals with all the complex tasks of abstracting the hardware such that the components of the mobile device such as Bluetooth, camera, and sensors can be accessed via Gecko. Thus, Gonk is responsible for exposing the features of the chipset to be used via the WebAPIs to Gecko.

Gecko – the engine

Gecko is the web engine that connects components such as HTML and JavaScript to the underlying low-level layer of Gecko. Gecko is the same HTML parsing and rendering engine that is used in the Firefox web browser. However, a certain web renderer of Gecko is used for this project just as different variants of Gecko are used for Firefox, Windows, Android, and OS X. Gecko is responsible for handling details such as providing access to the hardware via secure APIs. It consists of a robust security framework and it also handles the update management, along with various other core services. It is basically an application runtime layer.

Gaia – the interface

Gaia is the user interface part of Firefox OS. It is what we actually see in the OS. The app launcher and all the default applications such as camera, dialer, and settings are part of Gaia, and are completely built using HTML, CSS and JavaScript. This is the final layer of Firefox OS. Gaia exposes the WebAPIs for developers to interact with Gecko and the underlying hardware. As Firefox OS is completely open source and available online on GitHub (Gaia) and Mercurial (Gecko and Gonk), it gives full access to the user so that they can tweak the default look and feel of Firefox OS to suit their personal or organizational needs.

Firefox OS applications

Next are the third-party applications that are made by great developers like you and are running on Gaia. These applications run on top of Gaia and can be downloaded from the Firefox Marketplace. You will learn how to make these applications shortly after you study some essentials of Firefox OS.

The working of components under Firefox OS's hood – an example

Let's take the example of the camera application of Firefox OS. Let's think of a high-level view of what happens when we take a picture in Firefox OS's ecosystem. We open the **Camera** application, which is a part of Gaia. Gaia makes use of the Camera API, which is implemented in Gecko to run the application, as Gecko is the rendering engine for the operating system. Gecko then passes the requests to Gonk, which interfaces with the hardware. Gonk sends a low-level request to the chip that activates the camera and actually takes a picture.

> Note that the flow of control here goes from the highest layer in the abstraction layer to the lowest layer of the OS, and then finally to the mobile hardware.

All these types of access to the hardware are provided to the developer via the WebAPIs, so you don't actually have to think of or concern yourself with what lies under the hood. It feels great to drive a car, but having abstract knowledge of what actually lies under the hood can always prove to be useful.

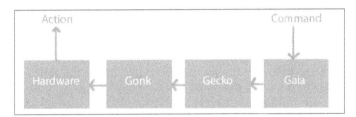

In the preceding illustration, the purple line from **Command** to **Action** denotes the flow of control from the highest to the lowest abstraction level, and finally to the hardware.

HTML5 and open web applications

Open web applications are those web applications that make use of open standard technologies, such as HTML5, CSS, JavaScript, and so on. These applications differ from native applications based on the fact that open web applications run on a web browser and hence can be accessed from a wide range of devices. These applications can be installed, access device hardware via the WebAPIs, and be run offline by making use of technologies such as AppCache and IndexedDB. However, these applications should be designed in such a way that they are cross-platform; if a device does not have all the hardware capabilities, then there will be a graceful degradation of the features of the application. Open web applications do not make use of proprietary technologies.

Let's take the example of Stack Edit (a web application), which is an online text editor that parses the markdown text and is very popular among authors. It is an example of an open web application. When loaded for the first time, it stores all its static data in the form of AppCache. All subsequent files that you store with the help of the in-browser text editor will be stored in the browser itself with IndexedDB. The application does not require a working Internet connection on subsequent runs.

The security model of Firefox OS

In Firefox OS, each application runs in an iframe with superpowers; hence, apps that run on Gecko run on a separate process that is a child process of the B2G system process. Due to this, a malicious application cannot disturb Gaia or other applications. Access to the underlying hardware is available only via the WebAPIs, which themselves are divided into different levels of permissions: Hosted (Web), Privileged, and Certified.

Each Firefox OS application has a manifest file that contains the details of the application. The developer has to declare the permissions for the use of the WebAPIs in the manifest file. Every application that runs in Firefox OS runs in a sandboxed environment. This means that the data generated by the application is sandboxed as well, and hence the data of one application cannot be accessed by another application. The following illustration will help you grasp the preceding discussion of application sandboxing:

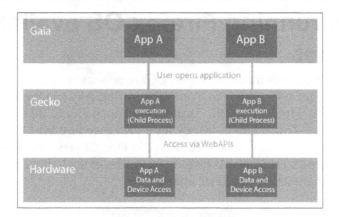

Even permissions from different websites are sandboxed on Firefox OS. For example, if an application uses OAuth to authenticate its users, then another app which uses a similar OAuth mechanism will ask for the login credentials again, even when you have used the login credentials in one application. This is because both applications are running in different sandboxes separately from one another, and the cookies of one application cannot be accessed by another application.

Don't worry if the concepts of the manifest file and the permissions levels are not clear yet; we will cover these topics in depth in *Chapter 3, Getting Your Hands Dirty: Firefox OS Apps*. Right now, you can just think of them as features that contribute to the application security in Firefox OS.

Firefox OS pays great attention to the user's data security as well. There is a setting called **Do Not Track** that helps to protect a user's privacy when browsing the Internet. The apps run in a sandboxed mode as described earlier, and once a user uninstalls an application, all the data associated with the application, such as cookies, AppCache, Local Storage, and IndexedDB, is also permanently deleted.

Devices running Firefox OS available in the market

A large number of devices that run Firefox OS are now available for purchase from many operators and carriers in over 30 countries. Alcatel One Touch Fire, LG Fireweb, ZTE Open, Huawei Y300II, Alcatel One Touch Fire C, ZTE Open C, ZTE Open II, Alcatel One Touch Fire E, Intex Cloud FX, Spice Fire MI FX1, Symphony Gofox F15, Alcatel One Touch Fire C 2G, Zen 105 Fire, Cherry Mobile Ace, Fx0, Orange Klif, and Spice Fire One MI FX2 are examples of such devices. The following image shows the newly launched Fx0 smartphone:

In 2015, Panasonic launched Panasonic CX700, which is a television that runs on Firefox OS. Isn't that amazing? Now, the applications that you develop can also run on televisions.

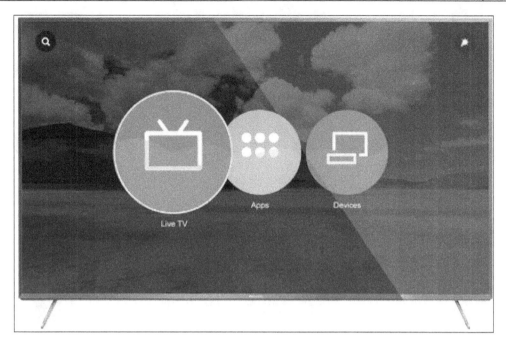

 For complete details of the specifications and availability of the various devices that run Firefox OS, you can visit the Mozilla Firefox OS devices website at `https://www.mozilla.org/en-US/firefox/os/devices/`.

Summary

In this chapter, you learned what Firefox OS is, why a developer should consider developing applications for Firefox OS, and the architecture and technical know-how of Firefox OS. We also took a look at the security model of the operating system, what open web applications are, and the devices available in the market that run Firefox OS. We looked at the devices on which our own applications will run in the future.

In the next chapter, we will study WebIDE, using which we will be able to run the Firefox OS simulator on our machines, as well as install and manage Firefox OS applications. We will go through the features of WebIDE and you will learn how to perform daily tasks on the operating system, such as uninstalling and browsing other runtime applications.

2
Running Firefox OS Simulators with WebIDE

In this chapter, you will learn how to use WebIDE and its features. We will start by installing Firefox OS simulators in the WebIDE so that we can run and test Firefox OS applications in it. Then, we will study how to install and create new applications with WebIDE. Finally, we will cover topics such as using developer tools for applications that run in WebIDE, and uninstalling applications in Firefox OS. In brief, we will go through the following topics:

- Getting to know about WebIDE
- Installing the Firefox OS Simulator
- Installing and creating new apps with WebIDE
- Using developer tools in WebIDE
- Uninstalling applications in Firefox OS

Introducing WebIDE

It is now time to have a peek at Firefox OS. You can test your applications in two ways: either by running them on a real device, or by running them in Firefox OS Simulator. Let's go ahead with the latter option since you might not have a Firefox OS device yet. We will use WebIDE, which comes preinstalled with Firefox, to accomplish this task.

 If you haven't installed Firefox yet, you can do so from https://www.mozilla.org/en-US/firefox/new/.

WebIDE allows you to install one or several runtimes (different versions) together. You can use WebIDE to install different types of application, debug them using Firefox's Developer Tools Suite, and edit the applications/manifest by using the built-in source editor.

After you install Firefox, open WebIDE. You can open it by navigating to **Tools | Web Developer | WebIDE**. Let's now take a look at the following screenshot of WebIDE:

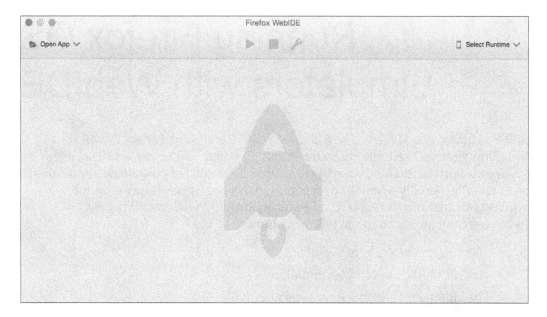

You will notice that on the top-right of the window, there is a **Select Runtime** option. When you click on it, you will see the **Install Simulator** option.

Select that option, and you will see a page titled **Extra Components**. It presents a list of Firefox OS simulators. We will install the latest stable and unstable versions of Firefox OS. We installed two versions of Firefox OS because we would need both the latest and stable versions to test our applications in the future.

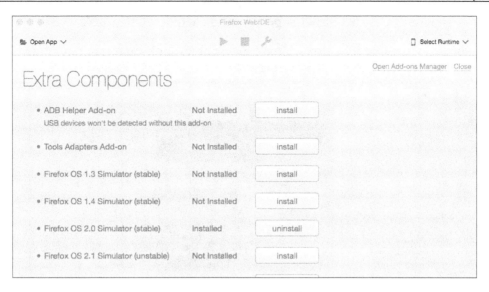

After you successfully install the simulators, click on **Select Runtime**. This will now show both of the OS versions listed, as shown in the following screenshot:

Let's open Firefox OS 3.0. This will open up a new window titled **B2G**.

You should now explore Firefox OS, take a look at its applications, and interact with them. It's all HTML, CSS and JavaScript. Wonderful, isn't it? Very soon, you will develop applications like these:

Installing and creating new apps by using WebIDE

To install or create a new application, click on **Open App** in the top-left corner of the WebIDE window. You will notice that there are three options: **New App**, **Open Packaged App**, and **Open Hosted App**. In Firefox OS ecosystems, there are two types of apps, Hosted and Packaged. We will study the difference between these two app types in detail in *Chapter 3, Getting Your Hands Dirty – Firefox OS Apps*.

For now, think of Hosted apps like websites that are served from a web server and are stored online in the server itself, but that can still use `appcache` and `indexeddb` to store all their assets and data offline, if desired. Packaged apps are distributed in a `.zip` format and they can be thought of as the source code of the website bundled and distributed in a ZIP file. Let's now head to the first option in the **Open App** menu, which is **New App**.

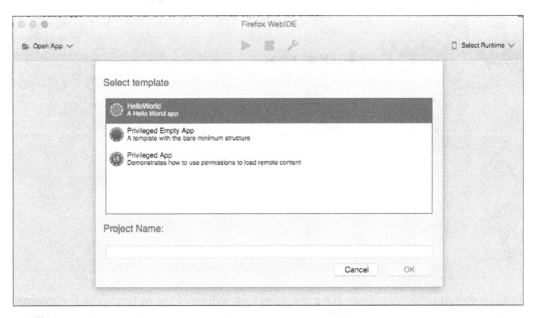

Select the **HelloWorld** template, enter a **Project Name,** and click on **OK**. After completing this, the WebIDE will ask you about the directory in which you want to store the application. I have made a new folder named **Hello World** for this purpose on the desktop. Now, click on **Open** button and finally, click again on the **OK** button. This will prepare your app and show details, such as the **Title**, **Icon**, **Description**, **Location**, and **App ID**, of your application.

Note that, beneath the app title, it says **Packaged Web**. Can you figure out why? As we discussed, it is because of the fact that we are not serving the application online, but from a packaged directory that holds its source code. This covers the right-hand side panel.

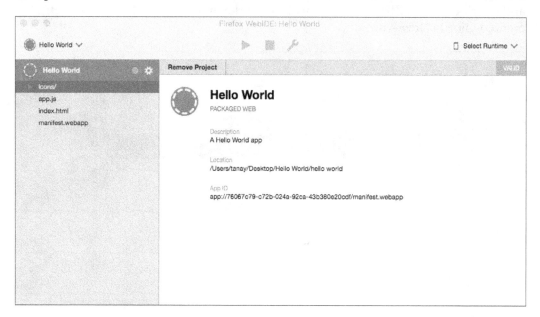

In the left-hand side panel, we have the directory listing of the application. It contains an icon folder that holds different-sized icons for different screen resolutions. It also contains the app.js file, which is the engine of the application and will contain the functionality of the application; index.html, which will contain the markup data for the application; and finally, the manifest.webapp file, which contains crucial information and various permissions about the application.

If you click on any filename, you will notice that the file opens in an in-browser editor where you can edit the files to make changes to your application and save them from here. Let's make some edits in the application— in app.js and index.html. I have replaced World with Firefox everywhere to make it Hello Firefox. Let's make the same changes in the manifest file. The manifest file contains details of your application, such as its name, description, launch path, icons, developer information, and permissions. These details are used to display information about your application in the WebIDE and Firefox Marketplace. The manifest file is in JSON format. We will study the manifest file in depth in *Chapter 3, Getting Your Hands Dirty – Firefox OS Apps*.

I went ahead and edited the developer information in the application as well, to include my name and my website. After saving all the files, you will notice that the information about the app in the WebIDE has changed! It's now time to run the application in Firefox OS. Click on **Select Runtime** and fire up Firefox OS 3.0. After it is launched, click on the **Play** button in the WebIDE, hovering on which is the prompt that says **Install** and **Run**. Doing this will install and launch the application on your simulator!

Congratulations, you have installed your first Firefox OS application!

Using developer tools in WebIDE

WebIDE allows you to use Firefox's awesome developer tools for applications that run in the Simulator via WebIDE as well. To use them, simply click on the **Settings** icon (which looks like a wrench) beside the **Install** and **Run** icons that you used to get the app installed and running. This icon says **Debug App** on hovering the cursor over it. Click on this to reveal developer tools for the app that is running via WebIDE.

Click on **Console**, and you will see the message **Hello Firefox**, which we gave as the input in `console.log()` in the `app.js` file. Note that it also specifies the app ID of our application while displaying **Hello Firefox**. You may have noticed in the preceding illustration that I sent a command via the console, `alert('Hello Firefox')`, and it simultaneously executed the instruction in the app running in the simulator.

As you may have noticed, Firefox OS customizes the look and feel of components, such as the alert box (this is browser based). Our application is running in an iframe in Gaia. Every app, including the keyboard application, runs in an iframe for security reasons. You should go through these tools to get the hang of the debugging capabilities if you haven't done so already! We will cover how to debug and test your Firefox OS applications extensively in *Chapter 7, Testing Your Firefox OS Application*.

One more important thing that you should keep in mind is that inline scripts (for example, `<a href="#" onclick="alert(this)">Click Me</a>`) are forbidden in Firefox OS apps, due to **Content Security Policy (CSP)** restrictions. CSP restrictions include the remote scripts, inline scripts, javascript URIs, function constructor, dynamic code execution, and plugins, such as Flash or Shockwave. Remote styles are also banned. Remote web workers and `eval()` operators are not allowed for security reasons and they show 400 error and security errors respectively upon usage.

You are warned about CSP violations when submitting your application to the Firefox OS Marketplace. CSP warnings in the validator will not have an impact whether your app is accepted into the Marketplace. However, if your app is privileged and violates the CSP, you will be asked to fix this issue in order to get your application accepted.

Browsing other runtime applications

You can also take a look at the source code of the preinstalled/runtime apps that are present in Firefox OS or Gaia, to be precise. For example, the following is an illustration that shows how to open them:

You can click on the **Hello World** button (in the same place where **Open App** used to exist), and this will show you the whole list of **Runtime Apps**, as shown in the preceding illustration. I clicked on the **Camera** application and it showed me the source code of its `main.js` file.

It's completely okay if you are daunted by the huge file. If you find these runtime applications interesting and want to contribute to them, then you can refer to the Mozilla Developer Network's articles on developing Gaia, which you can find at `https://developer.mozilla.org/en-US/Firefox_OS/Developing_Gaia`. Our application looks as follows in the App Launcher of the operating system:

Uninstalling applications in Firefox OS

You can remove the project from WebIDE by clicking on the **Remove Project** button on the home page of the application. However, this will not uninstall the application from Firefox OS Simulator. The uninstallation system of the operating system is quite similar to iOS. You just have to double tap in OS X to get the **Edit** screen, from which you can click on the cross button on the top-left of the app icon to uninstall the app.

You will then get a confirmation screen that warns you that all the data of the application will be deleted along with the app:

This will take you back to the **Edit** screen, where you can click on **Done** to get back to the home screen.

Summary

In this chapter, you learned about WebIDE, how to install Firefox OS Simulator in WebIDE, using Firefox OS and installing applications in it, and creating a skeleton application using WebIDE. You then learned how to use developer tools for applications that run in the simulator, browsing other preinstalled runtime applications present in Firefox OS. Finally, you learned about removing a project from WebIDE and uninstalling an application from the operating system.

In the next chapter, you will study packaged and hosted Firefox OS applications, the security levels of applications and application manifest files. You will then apply your acquired knowledge of Firefox OS applications to build an application called **Clickr**.

3
Getting Your Hands Dirty – Firefox OS Apps

In this chapter, we will start with an introduction to Firefox OS applications. You will then learn the difference between packaged and hosted applications, and the security access levels of different Firefox OS applications. Next, you will learn how to develop application manifest files for apps. Finally, we will conclude the chapter by building a simple Firefox OS application called **Clickr**, which checks the tapping speed of the user. We will go through the following topics in brief:

- Introduction to Firefox OS apps
- Packaged and hosted applications
- Security access levels (permissions)
- Application manifest files
- Building Clickr: A simple Firefox OS application
- Installing and running Clickr

Introducing Firefox OS apps

In this chapter, we will build a simple Firefox OS application, named Clickr, which is based on HTML5 and jQuery (a JavaScript library). Clickr measures the clicking/tapping speed of a user. A screenshot of this application is shown here:

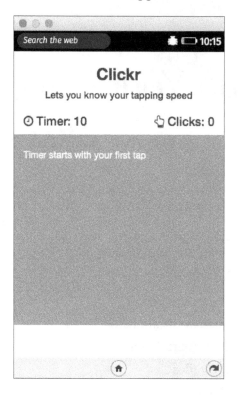

Let's first discuss the elementary difference between a web app and a Firefox OS application. The major difference lies in the fact that Firefox OS applications include a manifest file that contains the meta details and permission details of the Firefox OS application. These access Web APIs that allow the application to interact with the hardware. The manifest file provides the Firefox OS with the necessary information to install the application. As mentioned earlier, there are primarily two types of Firefox OS applications: packaged and hosted. Let's first understand the difference between these two types of applications and learn the advantages and disadvantages of using them. This will allow us to determine the application type that should be deployed in any given scenario.

Packaged and hosted applications

Packaged applications are distributed as zipped files whose content is delivered directly to the user's device. This is because packaged applications can access the Privileged and Certified Web APIs after being reviewed by the marketplace, and therefore can help in making the application more interactive with better device integration. The **startup** time of these applications is faster compared to hosted applications, because all the application's resources are loaded from the device itself, instead of being loaded from a remote web server. These applications work offline as well, unless the application requests data from a remote server. However, after the first load, a hosted app can be just as fast, provided that it makes use of offline technologies, such as AppCache and localStorage/IndexedDB. Packaged applications are different as they cannot be directly accessed through a URL. They take longer to be reviewed at the market place. Also, CSP is enforced on these applications, and if you wish to update your application, then you will have to upload it on the marketplace once again, and it will again, go through the review procedure.

Hosted applications, on the other hand, are served to a user's device from a remote web server, and the data is loaded from the web server every time the application is called, except when we use web technologies to make the application go offline. Hosted applications can also be published through the marketplace. Hosted applications cannot access the privileged and certified Web APIs. The **startup** time of these applications depend upon the network connection. These applications consume more data because the resources are not saved on the device by default (however, we can do so by making use of AppCache. You will learn more about how to do this in the next chapter). CSP is not enforced on these applications. If you wish to update your application, then you simply have to update it on the web server and the users will see the updated version of your application the next time they open it. Hosted applications can be distributed through both the official marketplace or through other channels, for instance, your personal website or a third-party marketplace.

The decision to build either a hosted app or a packaged app is a tough one, and it primarily depends on the type of application that you wish to build. The following illustration from the Mozilla Developer Network will help you in determining type of application to be used for your next application:

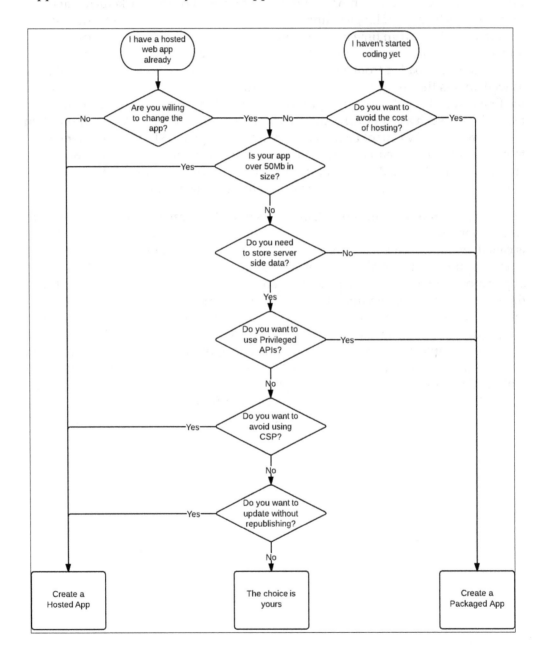

Security access levels (permissions)

Security access levels for Firefox OS Web APIs to access the device are divided into three categories, as mentioned earlier. Let's now study the three application types in detail:

- **Hosted apps**: These kind of apps have only on-demand permissions; they do not and cannot make use of the Privileged or Internal/Certified APIs. They can either be self published or distributed via the Firefox OS Marketplace after being digitally signed. The reviewing process of Web apps and Privileged or Internal Apps is different in the marketplace. These applications can be hosted applications as well. This is the default permission level of a Firefox OS application (by default type: web, if the type is not specified in the manifest file).

- **Privileged apps**: These kind of applications are apps that have permissions for device-sensitive APIs, such as contacts, browser, and so on. The type of application has to be declared as privileged in the manifest file of the application. Along with this, you have to declare every privileged Web API that you use under permissions in the manifest file. This information also helps Firefox Marketplace to review your application. Note that the review procedure of privileged apps takes more time than regular apps and these cannot be published outside of the Firefox Marketplace. As discussed in the previous chapter, CSP is enforced on these applications.

- **Internal/Certified apps**: These kinds of applications use the certified Web API which cannot be used by third-party applications. This is because an internal app must be approved by the OEM or Carrier. Currently, these apps can only be preloaded by the OEM and cannot be distributed in any other way. These applications have their type certified, and just as in the case of privileged apps, each and every internal Web API that is used has to be specified in permissions of the manifest file.

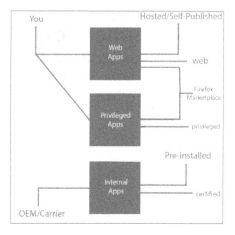

Building our application's manifest file

Now that you have studied the security access levels and the types of Firefox OS applications, we can get started with the construction of our app, Clickr. Let's first build the manifest file for our application. Our manifest file is fairly plain and simple since our application type is web and we aren't using any privileged APIs. We will build some fairly complex applications in the next chapters, and hence there will be other additions to their manifest files.

```json
{
    "version": "0.1.0",
    "name": "Clickr",
    "description": "An app to test your tapping speed",
    "launch_path": "/index.html",
    "icons": {
      "16": "/img/icons/icon_16.png",
      "48": "/img/icons/icon_48.png",
      "60": "/img/icons/icon_60.png",
      "128": "/img/icons/icon_128.png"
    },
    "developer": {
      "name": "Tanay Pant, Shubham Oli",
      "url": "http://stockwolf.net"
    },
    "default_locale": "en"
}
```

This manifest file isn't very different from what we made in our **Hello Firefox** application in the previous chapter. It is a JSON file that contains the regular information that every basic Firefox OS application should declare. Let's understand the various fields used in the manifest files, in detail.

Understanding the application's manifest files

As previously discussed, application manifest files are the key components that distinguish a website from a web application. The manifest files of applications are named manifest.webapp (it is crucial to use the .webapp extension for the Firefox OS to recognize the application type).

Some things must be taken care of when serving manifest files. These are listed as follows:

- App Manifests should be served with the content-type of application/x-web-app-manifest+json

- If you serve using the Apache web server, then you have to add the following line in your .htaccess file:

  ```
  AddType application/x-web-app-manifest+json .webapp
  ```

- The manifest file should be served from the same origin as the application

- The format of the JSON file should be correct; if it's not then the WebIDE will show an error

- The manifest file should be placed at the root directory of the application, and all the files whose locations are mentioned in the manifest should be relative to the location of the manifest file

- If you use external paths for resources in your manifest file then the URL should be in full and proper format along with http://

> Refer to the Mozilla Developer Network's documentation on App Manifest if you wish to know the details of all the required and optional fields. You can visit the following page:
>
> https://developer.mozilla.org/en-US/Apps/Build/Manifest

Directory structure of the application

Make sure your directory structure for the application looks like the following:

```
css/
  bootstrap.min.css
  style.css
img/
  icons/
    icon_128.png
    icon_60.png
    icon_48.png
    icon_16.png
js/
  bootstrap.min.js
  clickr.js
  jquery-1.11.3.min.js
index.html
manifest.webapp
```

We have used the icons taken from `http://www.iconarchive.com/` (commercial free license). These icons are displayed on the Firefox Marketplace with our application and also on the app launcher after the application is installed. Icons are used to add a visual distinctiveness to our application. You can see the icon that we have used is displayed with our application in WebIDE.

Constructing the index file

Let's now start with application construction. Apart from the manifest, the application consists of an `index.html` file for markup, and a `style.css` file in a folder named `css` for defining the style of the application. Icons are stored in the **icons** folder, which is inside another folder named `img`; the program logic is present in the `clickr.js` file in the `js` folder. We have used the Bootstrap UI Framework to handle the responsiveness and UI of the application. Also, we have used the Awesome font to display the icons inside the app, as well as the jQuery framework to help us handle the program logic.

You might have noticed that we have refrained from using inline CSS/JS code in order to respect the platform's CSP guidelines that we discussed earlier so that we do not face any CSP warnings. This helps us to make the web applications secure.

The structure of the index file is fairly simple. In the `<head>` section we have imported the various stylesheets and fonts. In the body, we have different components that include the heading text, a time counter along with a click counter, a tapping pad that displays the score, and a **Refresh** button, which appears when the time is up. Finally, we have called the various scripts to be imported in the end.

 Scripts are not placed in the header tag so that they load after the page has finished loading and don't hinder the loading process of the content of the page.

Here's the source code of the index file:

```html
<!DOCTYPE html>
<html>
<head>

  <title>Clickr</title>
  <meta name="viewport" content="width=device-width, initial-scale=1.0, maximum-scale=1.0, user-scalable=no"/>
  <link href="http://fonts.googleapis.com/css?family=Rancho&amp;effect=3d-float" rel="stylesheet"/>
  <link rel="stylesheet" href="css/bootstrap.min.css">
```

```
    <link rel="stylesheet" href="https://maxcdn.bootstrapcdn.com/font-
awesome/4.3.0/css/font-awesome.min.css">
    <link rel="stylesheet" href="css/style.css">

</head>
<body>

  <div class="container">
    <div class="row">
      <div class="col-md-12 text-center">
        <h3><b>Clickr</b></h3>
        <h5>Lets you know your tapping speed</h5>
      </div>
    </div>

    <div class="row">
      <div class="col-md-12">
        <h4>
          <div><i class="fa fa-clock-o"></i> Timer: <span
id="timer">10</span>
            <span class="pull-right">
              <i class="fa fa-hand-o-up"></i> Clicks: <span id="mouse-
clicks">0</span>
            </span>
          </div>
        </h4>
      </div>
    </div>

    <div class="row">
      <div class="col-md-12 clicking-pad">
        <br><span id="pad-text">Timer starts with your first tap</
span><br><br>
        <button id="restart-icon" class="btn btn-default"><i
class="fa fa-refresh"></i> Restart</button>
      </div>
    </div>
  </div>

  <script src="js/jquery-1.11.3.min.js"></script>
  <script src="js/bootstrap.min.js"></script>
  <script src="js/clickr.js"></script>

</body>
</html>
```

Constructing the stylesheet

Our stylesheet is fairly small and simple since we are using the bootstrap framework. We have simply defined custom styles for the clicking pad, and the text inside the clicking pad:

```css
/* stylesheet for clickr */

div.clicking-pad {

    height: 280px;
    background-color: #4CAF50;
}

#pad-text{

  color: white;
  background-color: #4CAF50;

}
```

Constructing the application logic

This is the JavaScript code that powers our Clickr application. As mentioned earlier, we have used the jQuery framework instead of vanilla JavaScript to make the application code shorter!

Here's the source code of the application's JavaScript file:

```javascript
/* Javascript file for clickr */

"use strict";

// some local variables
var clickr = {
  'clicks':0,
  'timer':null
};

( function() {
  // hides restart button initially
  $( '#restart-icon' ).hide();

  // binds click event to pad
  $( '.clicking-pad' ).on( 'click' , function() {
    if( clickr.clicks === 0 ){
      startTimer();
```

```
    }
    clickr.clicks++;

                $('#mouse-clicks').text( clickr.clicks );
    $('#pad-text').html('You have clicked
      <strong>'+clickr.clicks+'</strong> times');
  });

  $('#restart-icon').on('click',function(){
    window.location.reload();
  });
}() );
```

```
// startTimer function to start counter and update timer.

function startTimer() {
  clickr.timer = setInterval( changeTimer , 1000);
}
```

```
// function changeTimer to reduce counter by one.
function changeTimer() {
  var timeLeft = parseInt( $('#timer').text() );

  if( timeLeft === 0 ){
    clearInterval( clickr.timer );
    showResult();
  }
  else{
    $('#timer').text(( timeLeft - 1 ));
  }
}
```

```
// function showResult to show result after required time

function showResult() {

  $( '.clicking-pad' ).unbind( 'click' );

  var averageClick = ( clickr.clicks / 10 ).toFixed( 1 );

  $('#pad-text').append('<br>Average: <strong>'+ averageClick +
    '</strong> clicks per second');

  $('#restart-icon').fadeIn();

}
```

In the preceding JavaScript file, we have two local variables, clicks and timer, which we have set to zero and null respectively. We have used jQuery's hide() method to hide the **Restart** button when the page loads. We then have an onclick event that calls the function in case the number of clicks is zero, otherwise, it just increments the clicks variable. Then, we have used jQuery's text() and html() functions to display the value of our variables in the application. Finally, we click on the **Restart** button which reloads the page and hence, resets all of the counters.

The startTimer() function calls the changeTimer() function in 1000 milliseconds. This function handles the timer and calls the showResult() function when the time counter reaches zero. The showResult() function unbinds the click event from the clicking-pad element. We calculate clicks per second by dividing total clicks by 10 and making it an integer. We then append the details, such as clicks per second, by using the append() method to display the result in our application. We have used the jQuery fadeIn() animation to display the **Restart** icon when the game is over!

You can also make use of other frameworks, such as Angularjs, Emberjs or even vanilla JavaScript to create your application. Just make sure that the frameworks do not violate any CSP norms when you are using any new framework. Our application is now complete. We can run the application either as a packaged application or as a hosted application. Let's just run this as a packaged application for now.

Downloading the example code

You can download the example code files from your account at http://www.packtpub.com for all the Packt Publishing books you have purchased. If you purchased this book elsewhere, you can visit http://www.packtpub.com/support and register to have the files e-mailed directly to you.

Running our application on the simulator

Since we have finished building our first Firefox OS application, it's now time to run it and play with it. Follow the instructions that you studied earlier to open an application in the Firefox OS Simulator via WebIDE. After firing up WebIDE, open the application as a packaged application. You will see a window as shown in the following screenshot:

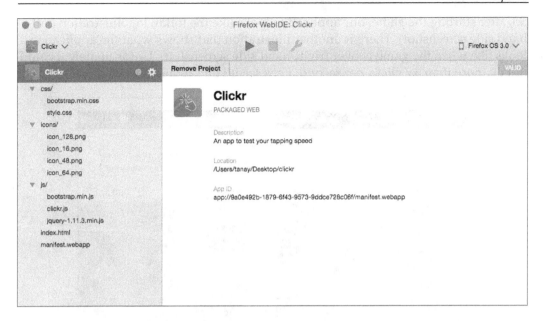

 The entire code of this application is located at GitHub under `tanay1337/Clickr`. You can also download the entire source code of the application as a ZIP file from:

`https://github.com/tanay1337/Clickr/archive/master.zip`.

You will notice that WebIDE has taken the details of our application and icon from the manifest file. Let's click on the **Install** and **Run** button (shaped like the play icon of your music player) to play with our application. Also, since our application type is Web (that is, we are not making use of any Privileged or Certified APIs) the description of our application is **PACKAGED WEB**. Had we used any privileged APIs in our application, we would have defined it in our manifest file, and the description would have read **PACKAGED PRIVILEGED**.

So, after starting the game, our application looks like the following illustration (left-hand side screenshot). There is another illustration that shows what the application looks like when the game is over (right-hand side screenshot). Unfortunately, I could not do more than 6.7 clicks per second. Let's see if you can get a better score!

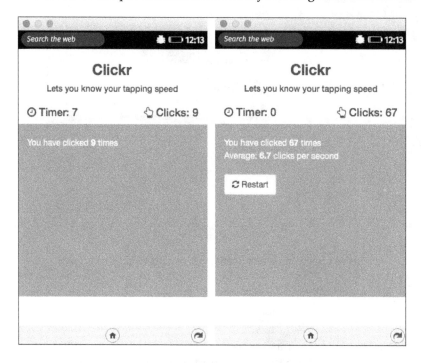

The application looks good, but don't you think that it would have looked better if the status bar, which shows the time and battery level, and the search bar weren't there? It is quite simple to get rid of these. You just have to add a single line to your manifest file to make this happen. Simply add the following to your manifest file:

```
"fullscreen": "true"
```

Now, reinstall the application by clicking on the **Install** and **Run** button (shaped like the play icon of your music player). This will now launch your application in full screen mode. The application looks much better this way.

Running the application as a hosted application

As promised, we will now run this application as a hosted application. For this purpose, I will use XAMPP for Mac OS X to create a web server that will allow me to serve the hosted application.

> XAMPP is also available for Windows and Linux; you can download XAMPP from `https://www.apachefriends.org/download.html`.

Let's place all the application files in the `htdocs` folder and start the apache server. This will allow us to see the application when we type either `localhost` or `127.0.0.1` in our web browser.

Now, open WebIDE and click on **New App.** Select **Open Hosted App**. This will ask you to enter the manifest URL of the hosted app. Go ahead and enter the manifest URL of your application, which should be `http://localhost/manifest.webapp`. This will open your application along with all of its details, in the WebIDE.

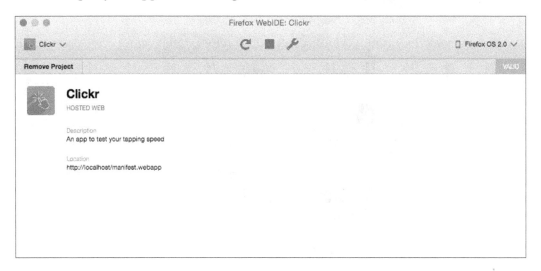

You will notice that the application type has now changed to **HOSTED WEB**. As you can probably figure out, this is because we are now serving our app from a web server. The location of the application is shown in the location of its manifest file. The application runs just like it was running earlier, but if we disconnect from the Internet, or in our case, to simulate a similar condition, switch off the server, the application will fail to load. The following illustration showcases the problem that takes place:

Congratulations, you just finished making your first functional Firefox OS application! You might feel that this application lacks certain things as compared to other applications that you have seen. Some things that need to be taken care of are the improvement of the user interface and the implementation of some extra functionalities, such as an **Install** button, in case of a scenario where the application will be served as a hosted application from a web server and not from the Firefox Marketplace.

Also, in the case where this application is hosted, the user of the application might have problems in accessing this application if they have an erratic Internet network. We will take care of these two problems in the next chapter by introducing an **Install** button in this application and making the hosted application work offline using AppCache.

Web APIs are a crucial part of any interactive Firefox OS application. These allow the applications to interact with the device, and hence make the applications more intuitive. We have also seen the different types of Web APIs, which are Web, Privileged, and Certified. We will use these Web APIs to improve our applications, and to make the applications more appealing and useful to the users. Web APIs are what make web applications comparable to the functionality of the native applications in other operating systems, like Android or iOS.

Summary

In this chapter, you learned about Firefox OS applications, the difference between hosted and packaged applications, and the different types of permissions of a Firefox OS application. You then studied the application manifest files, created a Firefox OS application named Clickr, made the application run on the simulator as a packaged application as well as a hosted application, and made the application fullscreen. We then built Clickr, and had a brief discussion on Web APIs.

In the next chapter, you will study how to make hosted applications installable and offline with the help of Application Cache. We will apply these features to Clickr. We will also build a Firefox OS application called "Check In!" (a geolocation tagging application) to implement the knowledge acquired by us.

4
Diving Deeper with the Fox Creating Richer Apps

In this chapter, you will learn how to make hosted Firefox OS applications installable. You will then learn how to make hosted applications work offline with the help of Application Cache. You will keep implementing the technologies that you have learned in Clickr. Finally, you will build Check In!, an application that will use several Web APIs to capture the user's position in a map, add comments, and save the information. This will help to improve your understanding of Firefox OS applications. We will go through the following topics in brief:

- Making hosted apps installable
- Making hosted apps offline with AppCache
- Building Check In! (a geolocation tagging app)
- Installing and testing Check In!

Making hosted applications installable

In this section, we will work on making our hosted application installable so that users who visit our application through the web browser on their Firefox OS mobiles are provided with an option to install the application on their phones, as shown in the following screenshot:

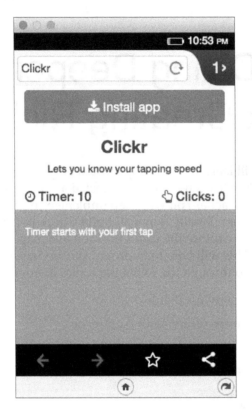

The **Install App** button will only show up if the user opens the application on Firefox OS. When the user loads the website on a desktop browser, we will keep the button hidden. We will also keep it hidden when the hosted web application that the user opens is already installed on their device.

We need to make changes in our clickr.js file in order to add the **Install** button. You will notice a new property under the **clickr** object named manifest_url that needs to be set to null. There is a new function called install(), where the variable installLocFind installs the application. If it returns a success, which means the application has been successfully installed, then it will hide the **install** button and call the initialisation function.

If some error occurs, for instance, if the user clicks on the **Cancel** button, it will execute an alert stating the reason why the application was not installed. Here's the JavaScript code for the application:

```javascript
var clickr = {

  'manifest_url': null,
  'clicks': 0,
  'timer': null

};

function install( ev ) {
  // to prevent the default action of the function (click)
  ev.preventDefault();

  // installs the app using API.
  var installLocFind = navigator.mozApps.install( clickr.manifest_url
);

  installLocFind.onsuccess = function() {

    $('.installer').hide();
    clickrFunc();
  }

  // if error occurs during installation
  installLocFind.onerror = function() {

    // App wasn't installed, info is here
    alert(installLocFind.error.name);
  }
}

( function() {

  // checks whether the OS is firefox OS.
  if (navigator.mozApps) {

    // firefox OS then show installer
    $('.installer').show();

    // define the path for manifest URL
    var path = location.href.split('/');
```

```
    // removes index.html from URL to get only path not trailing
filename
    path.pop();
    path = path.join("/") + "/";

    clickr.manifest_url =  path + 'manifest.webapp';

    // get a reference to the button and call install() on click if
the app isn't already installed. If it is, hide the button.

    var button = document.getElementById('install-btn');

    // checks whether app is installed or not
    var installCheck = navigator.mozApps.checkInstalled( clickr.
manifest_url );

    installCheck.onsuccess = function() {

        // if app is already installed.
        if( installCheck.result ) {

            // hides the install button.
            button.style.display = "none";

            // hides installer container.
            $('.installer').hide();
        }
        else {
            button.addEventListener('click', install, false);
        }
    }
    clickrFunc();
    }
    // if OS if not firefox OS.
    else {
        $('.installer').hide();
        clickrFunc();
    }
 }() );

function clickrFunc(){
    ...Old Code Except the three functions...
}
```

Now, we check to see if `navigator.mozApps` exists so that the **Install** option is displayed only when accessed from compatible software. If we successfully find `navigator.mozApps`, we will find that it shows the **Install** option (otherwise, the **Install** button is hidden, and the application is initialized). Now, what the code further does is it takes the URL of the web application, splits it into an array from the trailing slash and removes the elements after the trailing slash, appends a slash, and appends `manifest.webapp` (for example, if your URL is `http://localhost/index.html`, it will become `http://localhost/manifest.webapp`). This value will be saved in the `clickr.manifest_url` variable which was initially `null`.

The **Install App** button is defined by the variable button and `installCheck` checks whether the application is already installed or not. If it returns a `success`, it means that the application is already installed, in which case we will hide the install button. Otherwise, we will show the button with an event listener attached to it in the case of a click event it will install the application. Finally, the application will be initialized.

All our old code of `clickr.js`, except the three functions that were present in the previous version of the application, are now placed in the `clickrFunc()` function, which is our initialization function. The following screenshot shows what happens when we click on the **Install App** button of the web application:

Clicking on **Install** will install the application just as we used to install hosted applications via WebIDE. Let's click on **Cancel** instead and see what happens. We get a notice that warns us that even if we cancel the installation, we will not get a refund once the application is purchased. It again shows a confirmation box to either cancel the installation or resume the installation. Let's click on **Cancel Install**; this fires up our alert box stating the reason for failure of installation. We get a message called **DENIED**, which states that the user has denied our application the permission to be installed on their device. So, here we are with our first installable hosted Firefox OS Application. Now it's time to make our hosted app work offline with AppCache.

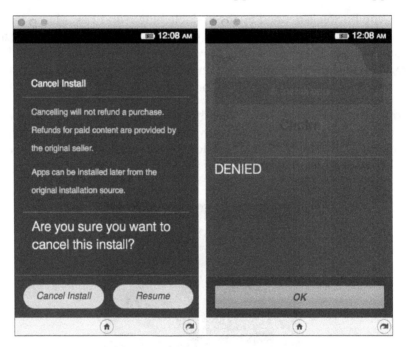

Making hosted apps work offline with AppCache

Wouldn't it be great if we didn't face network problems like the one we faced in the previous chapter? Then, for simple applications that do not use a data connection or privileged Web APIs, we could simply use hosted variants for distribution of without going through the Firefox Marketplace. There's a solution for this problem called **AppCache**. Using AppCache, we can make our applications work offline. The full form of AppCache is Application Cache and with the help of this, after the first time the application is loaded, no internet connection is required for the working of the application.

Application Cache is a component of HTML5 and is really very easy to implement. Implementing AppCache is as simple as including a `manifest.appcache` file in the root of your application. In the manifest file, you have to include the resources that you want the browser, or in our case the operating system, to cache. You can cache static resources, such as stylesheets, HTML documents, JavaScript files, and images. However, one thing that you should take care of while using AppCache is that you should never include the AppCache manifest file as well as the `manifest.webapp` file in the list of resources to be cached, as it will lead to a loop that will not allow your manifest files to be updated, even if you change the AppCache manifest. To enable AppCache on your website, you have to include the reference of the manifest file in the `html` tag of your webpage, as follows:

```
<html lang="en" manifest="manifest.appcache">
```

Let's now develop the AppCache manifest file for our application so that our application can work offline. One important thing to keep in mind is that once the resources mentioned in the manifest file are cached, they will always be loaded from the cache itself and not from the server, even if the network is available. So, a change in the manifest is required to trigger the redownload of the cache manifest and hence all the resources listed in it. We can update the manifest by making changes in the comments of the manifest file. Comments start with a hash for the manifest file format. Here's the cache manifest file for our application:

```
CACHE MANIFEST
# 13-07-2015 V0.1.0

/index.html
/css/bootstrap.min.css
/css/style.css
/img/icons/icon_16.png
/img/icons/icon_48.png
/img/icons/icon_64.png
/img/icons/icon_128.png
/js/bootstrap.min.js
/js/clickr.js
/js/jquery-1.11.3.min.js


NETWORK:
*
```

The structure of the cache manifest is similar to what we discussed above. You will notice that we added a network flag in the manifest file. We did so because noncached resources do not load on a cached page unless the network resources loading in the page are whitelisted under the network flags.

Let's create this file and put it next to the `manifest.webapp` file. Now, install the application as a hosted application in the simulator, turn off your web server, and restart the application. You will notice that this time, the operating system does not throw network errors and the application runs brilliantly.

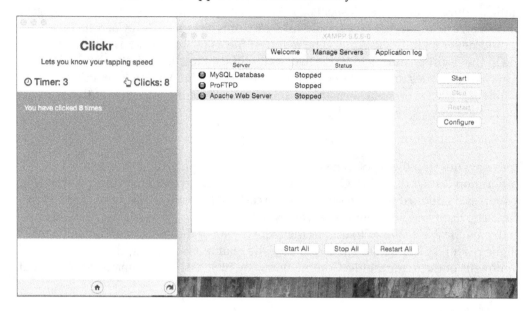

As you will notice in the preceding screenshot, I have my Apache Web Server off and yet the application is running smoothly. This is because all the resources that were required for the application to run have been cached by the operating system the very first time the application ran. So, for the subsequent runs, the network connection, or as in our case the web server connection, is not required!

Congratulations! You have finished building your offline hosted application. There are a few pitfalls associated with using AppCache that you need to be aware of. Apart from the precautions that I listed earlier, you need to remember that if a single resource listed in the manifest file is not found, then the loading process of the whole manifest file is dropped. Just like the App Manifest file, the cache manifest file must also be served from the same origin as the host and the files listed in the manifest are relative to the manifest file. If external URLs are used, then they must be in absolute form.

Building Check In!

We will now build a new application, called Check In! which allows users to log the locations they are in, along with notes/comments explaining what they are doing there. We will use two new WebAPIs namely Geolocation (for finding the location of the users and their devices) and IndexedDB (for storing the location and comments of the users).

We need to declare the application type as privileged in the manifest file and seek permissions in order to use the Geolocation WebAPI by mentioning it in the manifest file. So, let's write our manifest file first. As you can see in the following code, we can add permissions in the manifest file in regular JSON format by adding the name of the WebAPI we are using, along with the reason why the application needs to use the API. This information is used by Firefox Marketplace when reviewing your application, and by users when they are shown the connect screen when the applications access the API. Here's the manifest file for the Check In! application:

```
{
    "version": "0.1.0",
    "name": "Check In!",
    "description": "An app to log the locations you were in along with
notes/comments.",
    "launch_path": "/index.html",
    "icons": {
        "16": "/img/icons/icon16X16.png",
        "48": "/img/icons/icon48X48.png",
        "60": "/img/icons/icon60X60.png",
        "128": "/img/icons/icon128X128.png"
    },
    "developer": {
        "name": "Tanay Pant, Shubham Oli",
        "url": "http://stockwolf.net/"
    },
    "type": "privileged",
    "permissions": {
        "geolocation": {
            "description": "Obtain the current location of the user"
        }
    },
    "default_locale": "en"
}
```

The structure of the application Check In! looks like the following. We have put all the fonts in the packaged app to prevent CSP violations.

```
css/
    bootstrap.min.css
    font-awesome.min.css
    style.css

fonts/
    fontawesome-webfont.eot
    fontawesome-webfont.svg
    fontawesome-webfont.ttf
    fontawesome-webfont.woff
    FontAwesome.otf

img/
    icons/
        icon128X128.png
        icon16X16.png
        icon48X48.png
        icon60X60.png

js/
    app.js
    bootstrap.min.js
    jquery-1.10.2.js

index.html
manifest.webapp
```

Let's now develop the index.html file for our new application. The index page, as usual, is pretty straightforward. There is a header which shows the name of our application, along with an icon on all pages, and a container that houses the two buttons that show up in the landing page of our application. Then there is the main app container, where on clicking check in, you are shown your location on Google maps (in the mapHolder class) and where you can write notes and either save them or you go back to the landing page. There is also the prevMapHolder class, where you show the details screen of a previous saved entry. It contains the map holder and displays the description that you previously added.

Finally, there's the `viewAll` container which lists all your entries in a list in a concise format, upon clicking which you can see the detailed view for the application.

```html
<!DOCTYPE html>
<html>
<head>
  <meta charset="utf-8">
  <meta name="viewport" content="width=device-width">
  <link href='http://fonts.googleapis.com/css?family=Lato:100'
    rel='stylesheet' type='text/css'>
  <link rel="stylesheet" type="text/css" href="css/style.css">
  <link rel="stylesheet" type="text/css"
    href="css/bootstrap.min.css">
  <link rel="stylesheet" type="text/css" href="css/font-awesome.min.
css">
  <title>Check in</title>
</head>

<body>
  <div class="container-fluid">
    <div class="row">
      <div class="col-xs-12" id="title">
        <h1><i class="fa fa-thumb-tack"></i> Check In!</h1>
      </div>
    </div>
  </div>
  <div class="container checkIn">
    <div class="row">
      <div class="col-xs-12" id="btn-container">
        <button class="btn btn-primary btn-lg btn-block"
          id="checkIn-btn"><i class="fa fa-chevron-circle-
            right"></i> Check In!</button><br>
        <button class="btn btn-primary btn-lg btn-block"
          id="viewAll-btn"><i class="fa fa-location-arrow"></i>
            View All</button>
      </div>
    </div>
  </div>

  <div class="container mainApp">

    <div id="mapHolder">
```

```
      </div>
      <div>
        <h5><strong>What are you doing here?</strong></h5>
        <textarea class="form-control" id="notes" placeholder="Enter
          brief description"></textarea>
        <br>
        <div class="col-xs-12 text-center">
          <input type="submit" class="btn btn-primary"
            id="saveNotes" value="Save"> | <button class="btn btn-
              primary goBack"><i class="fa fa-chevron-circle-left"></i>
Back</button>
        </div>
      </div>
    </div>
    <div class="container prevMap">

      <div id="prevMapHolder">
      </div>

      <div>
        <h5><strong>You were doing</strong></h5>
        <div class="col-xs-12" id="showComment">
        </div>
        <br><br>
        <button class="btn btn-primary goBackList"><i class="fa fa-
          chevron-circle-left"></i> Back</button>
      </div>
    </div>
    <div class="container-fluid viewAll">
      <div class="row">
        <div class="col-xs-12">
          <h4><button class="btn btn-primary goBack"><i class="fa
            fa-chevron-circle-left"></i> Back</button> Previous
              Notes</h4><hr>
        </div>
        <div class="col-xs-12" id="prevList">
          <ul>
          </ul>
        </div>
      </div>
    </div>
```

```
<script src="js/jquery-1.10.2.js"></script>
<script src="js/bootstrap.min.js"></script>
<script src="js/app.js"></script>

</body>
</html>
```

Here's our small stylesheet to make some custom changes in the UI of the application. I would like to draw your attention to the fact that using Bootstrap has made our work very very easy, which is why we have such a small stylesheet where we have made just a few custom tweaks.

```
/* Stylesheet for Check In! */

div#btn-container{

  margin-top: 5%;

}
div#title{

  position: relative;
  top: 0;
  left: 0;
  background: purple;
  color: white;
}
div#googleMap{

  background: red;
}
div.mainApp{

  margin-top: 5%;
  width: 98%;
}
div#prevList ul{

  list-style-type: none;

}
div#prevList ul li{
```

```
    padding: 0.6em 0.8em;
    border-bottom: 1px solid RGB(128,128,128);
}
div#prevList ul li:hover{

    padding: 0.6em 0.8em;
    border-bottom: 1px solid RGB(128,128,128);
    background: RGB(230,230,230);
}
div#commentDisplay{

    margin-top: 5%;
}
```

Now, let's have a look at the home page of our application. So far, it looks quite good. We now have to deploy the actual engine under the chassis of our application, and that would be a gigantic (well, not that big) JavaScript file which we have named `app.js`.

It's now time to address the `app.js` file.

```
/* Javascript for Check In! */
```

Following the flow of control, we have some new variables that are initialized as `null` or `empty`.

```
var coords = {
   latitude: null,
   longitude: null,
   note: null,
   db: ''
};
```

Now, we have all the views other than the landing page view hidden by default. We now have a function called `initDB()`. The explanation of the function is given later. The `attachEventsToElements()` function is called immediately after the `initDB()` function. Now comes the options variable; `enableHighAccuracy` is set to `true`, which means that if a device has GPS hardware, it will make use of it, otherwise it will try to retrieve the location by using an Internet network; timeout instructs our application to wait for only five seconds in order to retrieve the location, and `maximumAge` suggests that, over time the page is refreshed and the application will get new position coordinates. Now we have two functions for success and error. The success function takes the latitudes and longitudes, concatenates them together, and then displays the location on Google Maps. Error functions post the error on the console in case of malfunctioning. We then call the Geolocation API which contains the `success` function, the `error` function and options variables.

```
( function(){

  $('.mainApp').hide();
  $('.viewAll').hide();
  $('.prevMap').hide();

  initDB();
  attachEventsToElements();

  var options = {
    enableHighAccuracy: true,
    timeout: 5000,
    maximumAge: 0
  };
```

```
function success(pos) {

  var crd = pos.coords;

  coords.latitude = crd.latitude;
  coords.longitude = crd.longitude;

  var latlon = coords.latitude + "," + coords.longitude;

  var img_url = "http://maps.googleapis.com/maps/api/staticmap?cente
r="+latlon+"&zoom=14&size=290x252&sensor=false";

  $("#mapHolder").html("<h4>You are here now </h4><img
    src='"+img_url+"'>");

}

function error(err) {
  console.warn('ERROR(' + err.code + '): ' + err.message);
}

navigator.geolocation.getCurrentPosition(success, error,
  options);
}() );

function attachEventsToElements(){

  $('#checkIn-btn').on('click', function(){

    $('.checkIn').hide( function(){

      $('.mainApp').fadeIn('fast');
      $('#notes').val('');

    });
  });

  $('#saveNotes').on('click', function(ev){

    ev.preventDefault();

    coords.note = $('#notes').val();
```

```
        saveNote();
    });

    $('.goBack').on('click', function(){

        $('.viewAll, .mainApp').hide( function(){

            $('.checkIn').fadeIn();
        });
    });

    $('.goBackList').on('click', function(){

        $('.prevMap').hide( function(){

            $('.viewAll').fadeIn();
        });
    });

    $('#viewAll-btn').on('click', function(){

        $('.checkIn').hide( function(){

            $('.viewAll').fadeIn();

            $('#prevList ul').html('');
            viewPrevious();
        });
    });
```

We then have a document.on call which loads the list of the previous locations that we saved in the database, along with the notes attached to them.

```
    $(document).on('click', '.list',  function(){

        var lat = parseFloat( $(this).find('.list_latitude').text() );
        var lon = parseFloat( $(this).find('.list_longitude').text() );
        var note = $(this).find('.list_note').text();
        var latlon = lat + "," + lon;
var img_url = "http://maps.googleapis.com/maps/api/staticmap?center="+
latlon+"&zoom=14&size=290x252&sensor=false";
```

```
     $("#prevMapHolder").html("<h4>You were here </h4><img src='"+img_
url+"'>");

     $('.viewAll').hide( function(){

       $('.prevMap').fadeIn();
     })

     $('#showComment').html('<em>'+note+'</em>');
   });
   return true;
}
```

As the name suggests, `attachEventsToElements()` function is a basic function that attaches events to buttons and clicks, and uses jQuery animations as well.

```
function initDB(){

   var request = indexedDB.open('notesdb', 1);

   request.onsuccess = function (e) {
     // e.target.result has the connection to the database
     coords.db = request.result;
   };

   request.onerror = function (e) {

       console.log("Creation error:"+ e);
   };

   request.onupgradeneeded = function (e) {

     // e.target.result holds the connection to database
     cords.db = e.target.result;

     if ( coords.db.objectStoreNames.contains("notes") ) {

       coords.db.deleteObjectStore("notes");
     }

     var objectStore = coords.db.createObjectStore('notes', { keyPath:
'id', autoIncrement: true });
   };
   return true;
}
```

What `initDB()` does is that it opens up a new database called `notesdb` in the OS/ browser. As usual, there are conditions related to the success and error of the function. If there is any error, then it will show up in the console, and this will help us to debug the application in future.

```
function saveNote(){

  var note = coords.note;
  var lat = coords.latitude;
  var lon = coords.longitude;

    // Handling addition of notes to db
    // the note
    var note = {'note':note, 'latitude':lat, 'longitude':lon};
    var transaction = coords.db.transaction([ 'notes' ], 'readwrite');

    // add the note to the store
    var store = transaction.objectStore('notes');

    var request = store.add(note);

    request.onsuccess = function (e) {

      alert("Your note has been saved");
    };

    request.onerror = function (e) {

      alert("Error in saving the note. Reason : " + e.value);
    };
}
```

Then comes the `saveNote()` function. This assigns the details obtained to some variables and passes the values of these variables in JSON format to store them in the notes table of our IndexedDB database named `notesdb`. It has success and error functions attached; in case of success, it shows an alert message that states *Your note has been saved* and in case of error, it shows an alert message that states *Error in saving the note. Reason: ...*, along with the reason in place of the three dots.

```
function viewPrevious(){

    var objectStore = coords.db.transaction("notes").
  objectStore("notes");
```

```
objectStore.openCursor().onsuccess = function(event) {

    var cursor = event.target.result;

    if (cursor) {

        if( ( cursor.value.latitude === null && typeof variable
        === "object" ) || ( cursor.value.longitude === null &&
        typeof cursor.value.longitude === "object" ) ){
        $('#prevList ul').append('<li class="list"><i
        class="fa fa-caret-square-o-right fa-3x pull-
        left"></i> <small>Lat.: <span
        class="list_latitude"><em>'+
        cursor.value.latitude+'</em></span>
           <strong>Lon.:
        </strong><span
        class="list_longitude"><em>'+cursor.value.longitude+'
        </em></span></small><br><strong>Note: </strong><span
        class="list_note">'+cursor.value.
          note+'</span></li>');

        }
        else{
        $('#prevList ul').append('<li class="list"><i class="fa
        fa-caret-square-o-right fa-3x pull-left"></i>
        <small>Lat.: <span
        class="list_latitude"><em>'+(cursor.value.latitude).
        toFixed(2)+'</em></span>    <strong>Lon.:
        </strong><span
class="list_longitude"><em>'+
(cursor.value.longitude).toFixed(2)+'</em></span></
small><br><strong>Note: </strong><span class="list_note">'+cursor.
value.note+'</span></li>');

        }
        cursor.continue();
    }
    };
}
```

 The markup above does not violate **CSP (Content Security Policy)**. We prefer to keep the code as shown in the preceding snippet for simplicity, since we are not focusing on the best practices here, but instead on building applications on Firefox OS.

Finally, there is the viewPrevious() function. This function is used to retrieve the previous entries stored in IndexedDB. First of all, it calls the transaction() function. We call this function when we need to add, retrieve, or modify data in the database. The transaction() function takes two arguments (although the second one is optional) and returns a transaction object. The first argument is a list of object stores that the transaction will span. You can pass an empty array if you want the transaction to span all object stores. Here, the second parameter to transaction function is absent, which means it is, by default, set to read mode. Then, we are calling our objectStore notes for transaction. This returns our objectStore that is notes. Now, we make use of the cursor to step through all the entries in our objectStore that is notes, so we use opencursor() to create one. On success, we call a function that creates <li> elements to show further details in the page. cursor.continue() statement is for iteration of the next entries. There is an if, else statement, which is used to separate null and floating values because I have used .toFixed(2), which works only for floating values not for null.

Installing and testing Check In!

Now that we have finished coding the engine of our application, let's install the application and test it. It is a packaged application and we will install it using WebIDE. You will notice that the app type is now packaged privileged. It's time to run the application on the simulator now.

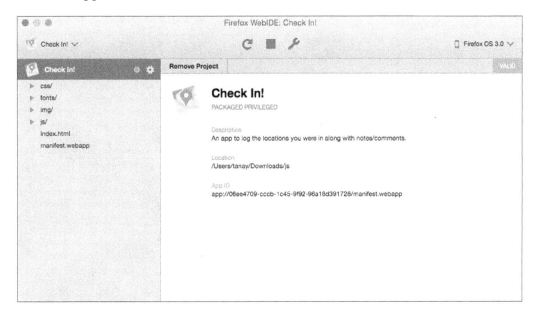

In the landing page, let's click on the **Check In!** button to see what happens. It shows me my precise location on the map and since I am at the mall right now, I will enter that and press the **Save** button. It gives me a confirmation on saving the **Check In!** that my note has been saved, as was expected.

Let's make use of the back button to go back to the landing page and view the saved entries. When we click on **View All**, we get the listing of our previously stored entries as shown in the following screenshot. When we click on an entry, we enter a detailed view where we can see our position during the time of our **Check In!** on a map as well as the note or memo that we saved during that time.

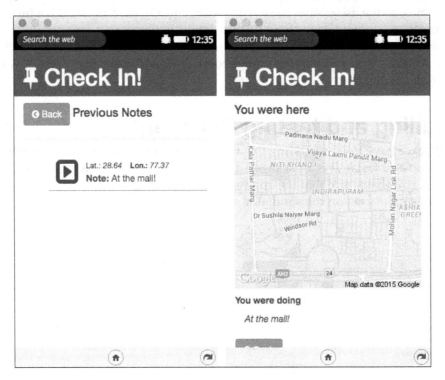

Also, you will notice that when you installed the application, it asked you for permissions via the permission screen as shown in the following screenshot. This was because of the specifications on our manifest file.

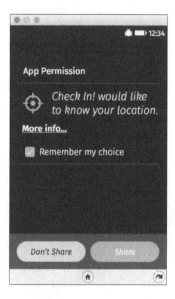

Summary

In this chapter, you have learned how to create **Install** buttons for hosted applications so that a hosted application that is not distributed via the marketplace can still be installed by the user. You also enabled hosted applications to work offline with the help of HTML5's AppCache. You finally built a new application called Check In!, that implements privileged as well as Web API to further strengthen your understanding of the process of application development for Firefox OS.

In the next chapter, you will learn how to make Firefox OS applications visually appealing, study basic design guidelines, and avoid UI blunders and learn about Gaia Building Blocks. You will then implement Gaia Building Blocks to Clickr while you learn to check the responsiveness of an application with the help of Firefox's Responsive Design View.

5
Making Applications Visually Appealing – Style Guide

In this chapter, you will learn some basic designing guidelines that will help you to make your application more user friendly. You will learn how to avoid some common UI blunders, and study Gaia Building Blocks. You will then implement Gaia Building Blocks to `Clickr` and check whether your application adapts to different screen sizes and resolutions with the help of responsive design view. We will go through the following topics in brief:

- Basic design guidelines
- Avoiding UI blunders
- Gaia building blocks
- Implementing Gaia Building Blocks to Clickr
- Checking design responsiveness with responsive design view

In this chapter, we will deal with topics such as how to make your Firefox OS applications visually appealing so that they share the look and feel of the Firefox OS default suite of applications, that is, the applications that are a part of Gaia. We will also discuss which practices should be followed while developing applications such as responsiveness. We will discuss the dos and don'ts of designing when it comes to developing mobile applications. We will also take a look at the usage of the Gaia Building Blocks. Gaia building blocks allow your application to share the look and feel of default Firefox OS applications.

We will update the UI of `Clickr` to prepare and deploy it to the Marketplace later on in this book. This updated UI will look similar to what is shown in the following illustration:

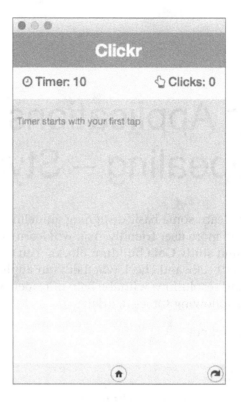

Basic design guidelines

Here are some basic designing guidelines that you should keep in mind while designing the UI layout for your application in order to offer your users a unique and intuitive app experience. The method of input should be carefully chosen in your application in such a way that typing is minimized. This helps the user of the application to enter data more easily (useful in mobiles with smaller displays). Think of unique ways in which your application can interact with the user, or ways in which the user can interact with your application. I must mention the example of Uber's mobile application which has done a great job in this regard. They use maps for the user to select their location instead of giving them textboxes to accomplish the same task. You should also think of alternate and innovative approaches to solve these problems.

The text displayed in the applications should be as concise as possible. Users might like to see an icon for the **Delete** option on their screen, rather than a block of text which says **Delete**. An approach like this not only saves the space on your screen but also makes your application look neater. Remember, a minimalistic approach to designing is good. Nobody likes a cluttered application with a ton of buttons on the screen. Also, your design implementations should be consistent throughout the application. This is because it will help to make your application easy-to-work-with for the users. For example, if the application uses the delete icon for deleting in one screen, then it should be the same everywhere. It shouldn't be like there's text in one screen and an icon in another.

To improve the bounce rate of your application, the launching page of your application should be really intuitive along with being neat enough to offer users what they want without having to read a help guide.

 For those of you who don't know what bounce rate is— it is the measure of how many people have moved on from your app after visiting the index page or the first page without continuing to any other screen/page of your application.

First impressions last, and hence the landing page of an application should be impressive. Important features should occupy prominent spots on your screen and should not be hidden in a clutter of graphics and page elements.

These basic yet immensely important guidelines should be followed when you create your application. Mozilla maintains a style guide for Firefox OS applications, which is quite useful and should be read by developers.

 You can read the guidelines here:
https://www.mozilla.org/en-US/styleguide/products/firefox-os/.

Avoiding UI blunders

There are some really common UI blunders that you should avoid making when coding the frontend of your application. Some of the commonly observed mistakes include developers do not realize that packaged apps do not have navigation options (back and forward buttons) like a regular web application opening in the Web browser.

Unless of course, you make them visible in the application by adding the following code to your manifest file.

```
"chrome" : { "navigation" : true }
```

This code runs your application in full screen and hides the status bar as well. Make sure that you have navigation controls in your application, preferably in the header so that your users do not get stuck in a page from where they cannot navigate to other locations in the application. The Firefox Marketplace will reject your application if things like this happen because Firefox OS devices do not have a back button.

Also, there are no zoom or search options in an app by default, since it's not opening in a browser. So you should include these features if your app needs these operations. For example, if your application is a document reader application, then users might want to increase the font size of the text to read it easily, or they might want to search for particular words or phrases in the document.

Never make the mistake of designing UI components too small; it is easy to interact with small elements in the WebIDE with a mouse, but in actuality fingers are much bigger and this can prove to be problematic. These are just a few common mistakes developers make that you should take care of while creating your application.

Also, make sure that your design is responsive so that your application can run easily on a wide range of devices such as smart televisions and smartphones with different screen sizes and resolutions. You can take the help of Bootstrap (http://getbootstrap.com), Foundation (http://foundation.zurb.com), or Materialize (http://materializecss.com) to do so.

Gaia Building Blocks

Gaia Building Blocks are reusable UI components that are used to build the UI for the apps in Gaia. They are also referred to as Firefox OS Building Blocks. Since Gaia is open source, you can use the same stylesheets for your Firefox OS applications and regular web apps. There are different stylesheets for different components in Gaia's GitHub repository under the Mozilla-b2g organization.

 You can access the style sheets on GitHub at https://github.com/mozilla-b2g/gaia/tree/master/shared/style.

You will notice that along with the stylesheets, there are directories with the same names as stylesheets, such as buttons, lists, and scrolling. These directories contain assets, such as images and HTML code fragments. You can simply copy these assets to your project in order to use them. You should also keep in mind that Gaia building blocks are not cross-browser compatible, and they don't work in Safari and Internet Explorer (compatibility problems in the Gaia Building Blocks are a shortcoming). So, you will have to put some extra efforts to take care of this in case you are building a hosted application, which is intended to run on other browsers as well.

Let's now implement Gaia Building Blocks on our first application, Clickr. You will notice two new files in the `css/` folder, `headers.css` and `buttons.css`. These files have been downloaded from the repository that I have mentioned earlier. Gaia building blocks have a different model of application, due to which we will have to make changes in `index.html` first. As you will notice, we first included both the `headers.css` and `buttons.css` in our html file. Then, in the body tag, we have used `role="application"` so that the Gaia Building Blocks can recognize the elements, such as headers and buttons, and replace them with the Gaia version of these elements. Also, we used section tags so that the application can see the content inside it as a different region. For this, we have used the `role="region" class="skin-comms"` attributes. The `skin-comms` class has been used to select a particular skin for the header that we have used. You will understand the significance of these changes in a much better way if you take a look at the CSS files.

```html
<!DOCTYPE html>
<html>
<head>

  <title>Clickr</title>

  <meta name="viewport" content="width=device-width, initial-scale=1.0, maximum-scale=1.0, user-scalable=no"/>

  <link href="http://fonts.googleapis.com/css?family=Rancho&amp;effect=3d-float" rel="stylesheet"/>
  <link rel="stylesheet" href="css/bootstrap.min.css">
  <link rel="stylesheet" href="css/buttons.css">
  <link rel="stylesheet" href="https://maxcdn.bootstrapcdn.com/font-awesome/4.3.0/css/font-awesome.min.css">
  <link rel="stylesheet" href="css/headers.css">
  <link rel="stylesheet" href="css/style.css">

</head>
```

```
<body role="application">

  <section role="region" class="skin-comms">
    <header>
      <h1 class="title"><em><b>Clickr</b></em></h1>
    </header>
  </section>
  <div class="container mainApp">
    <div class="row">
      <div class="col-md-12">
        <h4>
          <div class="stats"><i class="fa fa-clock-o"></i> Timer:
<span id="timer">10</span>
            <span class="pull-right">
              <i class="fa fa-hand-o-up"></i> Clicks: <span id="mouse-
clicks">0</span>
            </span>
          </div>
        </h4>
      </div>
    </div>
    <div class="row">
      <div class="col-md-12 clicking-pad">
        <br><span id="pad-text">Timer starts with your first
tap</span><br><br>
        <button id="restart-icon" class="recommend">Restart</button>
      </div>
    </div>
  </div>

  <script src="js/jquery-1.11.3.min.js"></script>
  <script src="js/bootstrap.min.js"></script>
  <script src="js/clickr.js"></script>

</body>
</html>
```

Also, we made a few changes to our `style.css` to match the color of the clicking-pad `div` and the text within it with the new look of the application. You will notice that I have made use of colors from the Firefox OS color palette style guide (`https://www.mozilla.org/en-US/styleguide/products/firefox-os/color/`) to select a suitable color for the **reset** button and the clicking pad division:

```
/* stylesheet for clickr */

body{

  background: RGB(250,250,250);
```

```
}
header .title{

  font-style: normal;
  text-align: left;

}
div.clicking-pad {

  height: 270px;
  background-color: #B2F2FF;
  padding-left: 2%;
  padding-top: 0.5%;
  margin-top: 2%;

}
div.stats{

  color: RGB(100,100,100);

}
#pad-text{

  color: #858585;
   background-color: #B2F2FF;

}
```

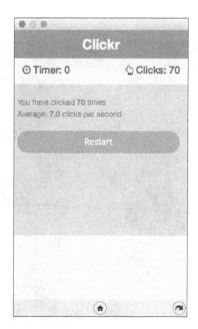

Checking responsiveness with responsive design view

As mentioned earlier, it is really important to thoroughly test if your application is design responsive. Earlier, developers had to take care of this task by resizing their browser windows, but thankfully, Firefox offers Responsive Design View in its arsenal of developer tools. You can go over to responsive design view by navigating to **Tools | Web Developer | Responsive Design View**. This allows you to check your applications by testing them in some preset sizes of mobile devices. You can also set a custom size by dragging the corners of the mobile responsive view to test the elements. It allows other options, such as displaying the page in landscape mode at the device size that you have set and simulating touch events. You can also take a screenshot of the application in the size that has been set by you by clicking on the camera icon.

The following is an illustration of our application **Clickr** in **Responsive Design Mode** set at size 320*480. You can go back to the normal view of the web page/application by clicking on the cross button present in the top-left corner of the **Responsive Design View** screen.

You can also enter the responsive design mode by pressing *Command + Shift + M* in your Mac.

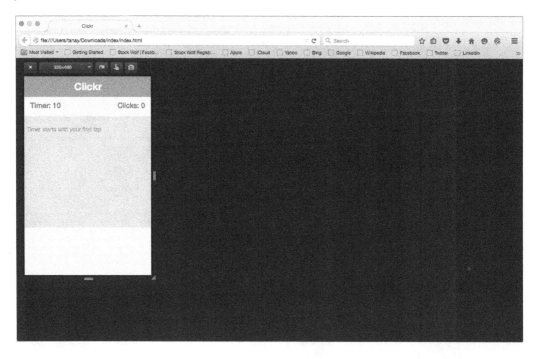

Summary

In this chapter, you learned how to design layouts for applications, some basic designing principles that should be kept in mind when designing an application's UI, avoiding some really common UI blunders, and about Gaia Building Blocks. You then applied Gaia Building Blocks to an application, and then finally used Firefox's responsive design view to test an application's responsiveness.

In the next chapter, you will study the WebAPIs and learn how to use them. You will also develop a photo-editing and sharing application making use of different Web APIs, which will help you to apply the knowledge that you have acquired so far.

Emerging a Guru – Learning Web APIs

In this chapter, you will learn about Web APIs, types of Web APIs and how to use them. You will learn to use them with the help of code samples. You will also study web activities, and you will finally implement all of your acquired knowledge to build FoxFoto, a photo editing and sharing application. We will go through the following topics in brief:

- Web APIs
- Types of Web API and their usage
- Web activities
- Using Web APIs in FoxFoto

This chapter that will take you through the core Web APIs of Firefox OS, has two major parts. In the first part of this chapter, you will study the various core Web APIs, and learn about their implementation and usage in brief. It will also cover various web activities (mozActivities) that are used for some native operations, such as pick, which is used for picking up images from the gallery and videos from SD cards or internal storage.

In the second part of this chapter, you will learn to use these APIs and Web Activities collectively, to create a feature-complete and fully-fledged app, FoxFoto. In this app, users will be able to select photos from a gallery, add cool effects to them, make a collage of the photos, tag them with a Geolocation (so that they can later see where the photos were taken), upload the edited photos to `http://imgur.com/`, and share the link with their friends.

Introducing Web APIs

Web APIs is a collective term used for various APIs that are available to JavaScript in the window context of a loaded HTML document. Firefox OS has additional Web APIs for hardware capabilities on smartphones and tablets, which do not usually exist on desktop or laptop computers. For example, the camera API can be used to open the camera of the device whenever required by a Firefox OS app. There are various APIs that have access to sensitive data, such as the contacts and settings API. Further in this chapter, you will study most of these APIs in detail.

According to Mozilla, there are more than 30 standard WebAPIs for Firefox OS. These APIs assist a developer to gain privileges for interacting with the hardware component of the device. For security purposes, not all of the APIs are open for developers to use in their projects directly, and these APIs require a certified level of permission. This permission is not for third-party developers, and is only available for OEMs and device manufacturers (built-in applications).

We need to specify the following permission levels in the manifest file (to use the APIs listed under them):

- **Certified level**: This permission is not available for third-party developers but only available for OEMs and device manufacturers. APIs such as Bluetooth and Web SMS require a certified permission to use them.

- **Privileged level**: This is given to every third-party developer, but after explicitly mentioning the usage of the API in the manifest file of the application. Applications made using this set of APIs come under privileged apps such as the contacts and device storage API.

Web and Privileged APIs

In this section, you will study the APIs which come under the web and privileged permission level, and are easily available for any third-party developer to use in their projects (but only after explicitly mentioning the application type in the app's manifest file for privileged APIs). Some of the web and privileged APIs are as follows:

- **Network information API**: This API is used to obtain information about the network to which the device is currently connected. This information can be about network speed or data usage.

The following code snippet detects the changes in user's connection and changes in logs in the console. It tells you about whether the connection is **wifi** or **cellular**:

```
var connection = navigator.mozConnection;
var type = connection.type;
// this function is called when there is any change in
connection
function updateConnectionStatus() {
  console.log("Connection type is change from " + type + "
    to " + connection.type);
}
connection.addEventListener('typechange',
updateConnectionStatus);
```

- **TCP socket API (Privileged)**: This API lets you manage and provide low-level support to TCP and SSL protocol. It also allows developers to play with protocols available over TCP, such as HTTP, IMAP, and so on.

  To open a connection, use the following method:

```
var skt = navigator.mozTCPSocket.open('localhost', 8080);
this opens a socket in localhost:8080, to listen to the
port use the following
var skt = navigator.mozTCPSocket.listen(8080);
and to send data (buffered data) use the following
skt.send(data);
```

  After you have sent and received the data, if you want to close the connection, simply use the `socket.close()` function.

- **Ambient light sensor API**: This API is used to detect ambient light levels near the device. It can be quite helpful as it detects the light intensity near the device and changes the brightness of the UI accordingly.

- **Battery status API**: This API provides you with information about battery related information, such as battery percentage, charging status, and so on. This API comes in handy when you want your app to run in minimum resources after the battery falls down to a certain level. You can use the following code snippet to test this API:

```
navigator.getBattery().then(function(battery) {
  // use this battery object to get various values.
}
```

The battery and charging status returns Boolean values. `battery.level` returns the level of the battery between 0 and 1.

- **Geolocation API**: You have already used this API, in the Check In! app. It gives you the latitude and longitude from where the device is currently used. It uses the device's GPS or Internet connection (from the IP address).

- **Pointer lock API**: If you are building a gaming application and want to lock the pointer, then this API will prove to be quite helpful for you. It also gives you access to the movement deltas rather than the absolute positioning of the pointer. For example, it is useful for first person 3D games.

- **Proximity API**: With the help of this API, you can efficiently use the device's proximity sensor. It helps the application to know when a user is close to the device. You have already seen its usage in the native dialer app, as when you are making a call, it automatically turns the display off.

- **Device orientation API**: This API notifies you regarding any change in the device orientation in context to the gravitational pull. It can be used to automatically rotate the view of the app to match the user's point of view.

- **Screen orientation API**: This notifies you about any change in the orientation of the screen from portrait to landscape and vice-versa, as screen orientation change is automatic. This can be used to set your app's preferred orientation. You can also lock screen orientation to avoid forced changing of the screen orientation just by declaring `orientation: "portrait"` to the fixed portrait layout for your app in the manifest file (orientation takes other parameters as well, such as landscape, landscape-primary, portrait-secondary, and so on).

- **Vibration API**: This is used when you need the device to vibrate to notify the user about something. For example, you can use this in games when the user tries to gain access to blocked levels. You can make your app vibrate by simply using the following code:

```
window.navigator.vibrate(200);
```

To stop the vibration, use the following code:

```
window.navigator.vibrate(0);
```

- **Web FM API**: This enables support for the device's in-built FM radio, if any, installed in the device. It allows you to turn the radio on/off, and switch between different radio stations. It also allows the functionality to automatically seek available channels.

- **File Handle API**: This is a nonstandard API, which means it is not fully supported by all devices and all Firefox OS versions. It gives you access to writeable files with a locking facility. It also allows manipulation and creation of files.

A detailed explanation of this API can be found at
`https://developer.mozilla.org/en-US/docs/Web/API/`
`File_Handle_API`.

- **indexedDB**: This is the same API that you used in the Check In! app. It is also the similar as the indexedDB API of HTML5. This API provides you with a database right inside your browser and can be used to save various information for faster retrieval.

- **Contacts API (Privileged)**: The user's contact book can be accessed by using the contacts API. The API can also be used to add, read, and modify the user's contact list.

The contact API can be used as shown in the following code:

```
var contactData = {
  givenName: ["Tanay"],
  familyName: ["Pant"],
  nickname: ["The Last Dragon"]
};
var contact = new mozContact(contactData);
var saving = navigator.mozContacts.save( contact );

saving.onsuccess = function() {
  console.log('Contact saved successfully');
};
```

- **Device Storage API (Privileged)**: This allows applications to add, read, and modify files, such as photos stored in the `images` folder, that are stored in the internal storage of the device. It is used to access the filesystem within the app.

- **Alarm API**: This allows you to schedule alarms or notifications for specific times, or launch an application after a specific period of time.

 Note that this API is more like `setTimeout`, but survives application and device restarts.

The following code schedules an alarm:

```
// The date to schedule the alarm
var date  = new Date("August 08, 2015 2:00:00");

// This is the message shown when alarm starts
var data  = {
```

```
    foo: "bar"
}

// The "ignoreTimezone" string makes the alarm time-zone
independent,
    means 2:00 p.m. same whether it is U.S or India

var request = navigator.mozAlarms.add(date,
"ignoreTimezone", data);

request.onsuccess = function () {
  console.log("The alarm has been successfully added");
};
```

- **Simple PUSH API**: This API lets you send notifications from specific applications. The `push` is an event that allows you to send notifications from a remote server to our device. These notifications are shown in the notification bar of our device.

- **Web notifications API**: This allows apps to send notifications that can be displayed at the system level. Sometimes, you want to display notifications at the system level, which means that instead of displaying a notification in the application, the notification bar is used to display the message. This API helps you in serving that purpose.

- **Apps API**: This API provides support for installing and managing web apps, and in addition to this, it allows applications to determine payment information.

- **Web activities API**: When a web app wants another app to perform an activity, we use this API. You can find more information about web activities in the next section that is dedicated to mozActivity.

- **WebPayment API**: This API allows web content to initiate payments and refunds in exchange for virtual goods. It is an in-app payment functionality. To use this API, you need to upload your app to Firefox Marketplace under the paid/in-app category and in return, you will get an application key and an application secret. For testing purposes, you can get credentials to test in-app payments.

 More details can be found here: `https://developer.mozilla.org/en-US/Marketplace/Monetization/In-app_payments_section/mozPay_iap`.

- **Browser API (Privileged)**: This API is used to build a browser using native components means, a web browser running inside a browser. This API needs the usage of iframes to embed the content by making iframe a top-level node inside document. With advance usage of this API, you can build a fully functional browser.

That's all for Privileged APIs; with clever and collaborative usage of the aforementioned APIs, one can build a real-world smart application.

Certified APIs

As you know, certified APIs are not currently intended for third-party developers but only available for OEMs and device manufacturers; therefore, in this section, you will learn about all certified APIs, but we will not go into the details of any of these, as we cannot implement them. The following Web APIs are listed under certified APIs:

- **Bluetooth API**: This gives us access to the device's Bluetooth hardware.

- **Mobile connection**: This provides us with information about the device cellular connectivity, signal strength, operator, and so on.

- **Network stats API**: This provides us with critical information about network monitoring, data usages and can expose this data to any application.

- **Telephony**: This allows the app to place and answer phone calls using the device's native system.

- **WebSMS**: This gives us access to read, delete, and create SMSs using an in-built messaging environment.

- **Wi-Fi information**: This provides us with information about the current Wi-Fi connection(s), signal strength, bandwidth, and all nearby available connections as well as connect, save, and forget connections.

- **Camera API**: This allows the app to take photos or make videos using the device's in-built camera.

- **Power management API**: This allows the app to switch the screen on and off, or limit the CPU power when in need of power management.

- **Settings API**: This allows the app to create and modify system-wide configuration values.

- **Idle API**: This ensures that apps can receive events, even if the user is not active for a longer period than expected.

- **Permission API**: This helps us to manage apps permission in centralized locations as defined earlier in the device settings.

- **Time/clock API**: This allows apps to set the current time. Time zones can be set by the settings API.

Web activities

Apart from the WebAPIs, there are certain Web Activities which allow our app to communicate with another application to perform certain tasks, such as pick, which is one of the most frequently used mozActivity. It is used to pick images from a gallery or capture fresh ones from a camera. You can write your own code to access the photo from the device storage instead of using pick activity. However, it is generally used to provide a common user experience for app-to-app interactions, and also to provide native hardware access (as in camera). Inter-app task delegation can also be performed using web activities. If you want to send an e-mail, then you would not program the functionality of e-mail using server-side languages, instead, you would use a new web activity to create a new e-mail using the default e-mail application or any third-party application that is installed in the device.

All the actions that these activities perform are chosen by the user. The user has to choose between built-in or third-party apps in order to perform the desired task.

Let's have a brief look at some of the web activities. The syntax is as follows:

```
var activity = new MozActivity({
  // we are using here pick to pick images of .png and .jpg type
name:"pick",
  data: {
type: ["image/png", "image/jpg"],
  }
});
// after successful completion
activity.onsuccess = function(){
  // perform some task after successful completion
  console.log( "Done!" );
};
// on encountering any error
activity.onerror = function(){
  // display error in more succinct way
  console.log( this.error );

};
```

The preceding syntax is sufficient for normal usage and you just have to change the name and data in the preceding code to use a different web activity. There are around 15 activities for Firefox OS, and we are going to have a look at some of them in the following table:

Name	Data filters	Description
browse	`type: "photos"`	Mainly used to browse photos or any other files inside a gallery.
configure	`target: "device"`	Used to configure the settings of a device.

dial	`type: "webtelephony/ number",`
	
	`number: +91-xxxxxxxxxx`
		It is used when an app wants to place a phone call.

new	`type: "webcontacts/ contact"`
	
	`type: "mail"`
	
	`type: "websms/sms"`
		Added in Firefox 2.0. It is used to create a new contact entry.
		
		It is used when an app wants to send an e-mail.
		
		Used when an app wants to send a SMS.

open	`type: [ "data/type1", "data/type2"]` data can be audio, video or image and type is `.mp3`, `.jpg`, `.mp4`, and so on.	Used to open a certain file of the desired type.

pick	`type: "image/png"`
	
	`type: "webcontacts/ contact",`
	
	`fullContact: "true"`
		Already been discussed.
		
		Added in Firefox 2.0, used to retrieve full contact information from the user's contacts.

record	`type: ["photos", "videos"]`	It allows the user to record videos or capture images.

Save-bookmark	`type: "url",`
	
	`url: {`
	
	`required: true,`
	
	`regexp: /^https?:/`
	
	`}`
		This saves a bookmark.

Name	Data filters	Description
share	`number: 1` `type: "image/*"`	To share through Bluetooth. When an app wants to share an image through email or set as wallpaper.
view	`type: "application/` `pdf"`	Used when an app wants to display the content of a PDF document. There are various other types of usage of this activity.
update	`type: "webcontacts/` `contact"`	It is used when an app wants to update a pre-listed contact.

These activities make life easier for developers. Instead of creating server-side logic (as we do in web apps), we mainly focus on an app's front-end logic and leave these side-by-side tasks to be done by other apps.

 The full description and documentation about the aforementioned WebAPIs and Web Activities can be found at `https://developer.mozilla.org/en-US/docs/WebAPI` and `https://developer.mozilla.org/en-US/docs/Web/API/Web_Activities`.

Building FoxFoto

After going through the extensive set of mind-boggling Web APIs and activities, it's the perfect time to get our hands dirty by building an app which uses these APIs and activities collaboratively.

The application which we are going to develop is an app that edits and shares images, with additional features to create collages from different images.

The HTML file

Let's now take a look at the HTML file present at GitHub for this application from the following link: `https://github.com/tanay1337/FoxFoto`.

This HTML code gives you the basic markup of the app, but without the use of CSS, it generates just a pale UI.

 Due to the space limitations of the book, full code of CSS is not shown here. The complete CSS code file can be found at `https://github.com/tanay1337/FoxFoto`.

After the implementation of CSS from the preceding link, the UI can be seen, as shown in the following screenshot:

The UI shifts from pale black and white text to a sleek and intuitive version. CSS is also quite helpful in designing animations (using Keyframes) without using any JavaScript or any of its libraries. There is a predefined set of CSS animations known as `animate.css` (`https://daneden.github.io/animate.css/`), which we have used in this app for smooth transitions from one screen of the application to another.

The complete JavaScript code for this application is quite long, so it will be explained as per the requirements (not all together, but in chunks at a time). The complete commented JS file can be found at the GitHub repository for this application.

The underlying JavaScript code

Let's now study the underlying JavaScript code that drives our application.

```
/* Javascript file for app */

"use strict";
```

First of all, we declare use strict to run the JavaScript code in strict mode. The strict mode insures our code against various syntactical errors. It is a good practice to always run your code in strict mode to avoid future exceptions.

```
// Some variables
var localVar = {
                 userLocation:null,      // to store user's location
                 imgCounter:0,           // to get no. of images
                   picked by user
                 imgurLink:null,
                 db:null,
                 canvasHeight:null,
                 image:{
                   img:[]
                 },
                 tmp:1,
                 lastLoc:0
};

( function(){
  // hides unnecessary elements
  $('#backBtn').hide();
  $('section.collageSection').hide();
  $('section.editImageSection').hide();
  $('#actionBtns').hide();
  $('#actionBtns2').hide();
  $('section.previousEdited').hide();
  $('#wantLocationBtn').bootstrapSwitch({size:'mini',onText:'<i
    class="fa fa-check"></i>',offText:'<i class="fa fa-
      times"></i>'});
```

Next, we define a set of local variables with the identifier `localVar`; this variable will be used as a global variable for various functions, but ultimately living in a local scope. Then comes our self-initialized function that will be invoked immediately as the code runs. Inside this function, we hide some of the unnecessary elements that are of no need at the initial phase.

```
// Setting options for Geolocation
var options = {
                enableHighAccuracy: true,
                timeout: 5000,
                maximumAge: 0
};

// Geolocation API call
navigator.geolocation.getCurrentPosition(locationSuccess,
  locationError, options);

// Call to initialize the DB
fireDB();

// function to call
attachEventsToAll();

}() );
```

Next, we call three functions, namely `navigator.geolocation.getCurrentPosition()`, `fireDB()`, and `attachEventsToAll()`. The first one is used to retrieve the current location of the device (Geolocation API). We have already used this function in our Check In! app. The next function that we call is `fireDB()` function, which is also the same as we used in our Check In! app. Finally, we call the `attachEventsToAll()` function which attaches events, such as click, hover, and so on, to various elements. The code for `attachEventsToAll()` can be seen by downloading the full JS (`app.js`).

After you have downloaded the file, you can see that click events is attached to various elements. You will see the addition and removal of classes like `animated`, `bounceInRight`, and so on. These are the classes that give the app's back and forth transition a sleeker and smoother touch.

These classes are defined in the `animated.css` file. Now, let's take a look at the code of the function that will be executed when the click event is fired on the `#pickImage` element. The code is as follows:

```
$("#pickImage").on('click',function(){

    // registering new mozActivity to pick image file
    var pickImageActivity = new MozActivity({
                            name: "pick",
                            data: {
                                    type: ["image/png",
                                        "image/jpg",
                                            "image/jpeg"]
                                }
    });


    // if image successfully picked
    pickImageActivity.onsuccess = function() {


        // styling canvas

        var img = new Image();
        img.crossOrigin = "Anonymous"; // enables cross origin
            resource sharing (CORS)
                // loading image with picked up image
        img.src = window.URL.createObjectURL( this.result.blob );

        img.onload = function(){
    var tmp = localVar.tmp;
            localVar.image.img[tmp-1] = img;
    // to maintain aspect ratio of the image
            var ratio = ((window.innerWidth - 20)/2) / img.width;
            var height = img.height * ratio;
            $('#imgDisplay').html('<p class="text-center"><strong>You
                Picked '+tmp+' images</strong>');
```

 We have made use of a certain component called bootstrap switch, which might cause a CSP warning (not error).

```
    if( tmp===1 ){
      localVar.canvasHeight = height;
    }
    else if( tmp%2==0 ){
      if( height >= localVar.canvasHeight ){
        localVar.canvasHeight = height;


      }



    }
    else{

      localVar.canvasHeight += height;
    }

    localVar.imgCounter++;

    if( localVar.imgCounter===2 ){
      $('#createCollage').show();
    }
    localVar.tmp++;

  };

};

pickImageActivity.onerror = function() {

  alert("unable to Pick Foto");

};

});
```

This code is executed when you click on the **Pick Fotos** button inside the **Create Collage** section. First of all, this code registers a new mozActivity pick as defined in the previous section of Web APIs and activities. This activity is used to pick images of the types `.png`, `.jpg`, and `.jpeg` from the user's gallery, or to capture fresh images from the camera. To make a collage, you need to select a minimum of two images; there is no upper limit. Although this is a very basic app that creates a collage; for a novice user of the canvas API of HTML5, it is more than enough.

As you can see, there is a switch which is marked off. This switch is used to include your current location as an image in your collage by fetching a static image of your location's map from the Google Maps API. Initially, this switch is turned off so, if you want to include your location in the collage, you need to turn it on.

Now, what's happening here after the successful picking of an image from the user's gallery or the camera? The onsuccess function gets fired and inside this function a new image object is created, and its crossOrigin attribute is set to anonymous to allow **CORS (Cross Origin Resource Sharing)**. This means that the image can be shared across other domains that were initially blocked for security concerns. The src attribute of this image object is set to what we got from the user's selection (this result is stored in this.result.blob). After the image is successfully loaded from src, a function is again fired, which stores the image object along with all its properties in an array that is defined under localVar.image.img[]. After storing the image object in an array, we set the aspect ratio of the image in such a way that, after resizing it does not get distorted. Now, after calculating the ratio, it is multiplied with height to convert the height of the image in same ratio as of width to maintain the aspect ratio of the image.

The next line displays the number of images that you have picked from the gallery or the camera. Now comes the tricky part, as you select images, the `localVar.` `canvasHeight` variable stores the total height so that when you click on the **Create Collage** button, a canvas of sufficient height should be drawn to fit all images. This is because you can't change the height of the canvas dynamically without it being redrawn. So for the first image it sets `localVar.canvasHeight` equal to the height of first image, then for second image it checks whether the height of the image of the second column is greater than the image on the first column of same row. If it is greater, `localVar.canvsaHeight` is set equal to the height of the image of the second column. This is done for all images that you pick. It increments the `localvar.imgCounter` variable by one to count the number of images you have picked and displays the **Create Collage** button after you picked up at least two images. There is a function to handle any errors that occur when the user's picks an image.

Next is the description of code that is executed when you click on the **Create Collage** button after you have picked up at least two images. Let's have a look at the following code:

```
// Attaching click handler to create Collage button inside Collage
Section
  $("#createCollage").on('click',function(){

    $('#pickImage').hide();
    $('.locationSwitch').hide();
    var myCanvas = document.getElementById("displayCanvas");
    $(myCanvas).show();
     // get total that user selected.
    var totalImages = localVar.image.img.length;

    if( $('#wantLocationBtn').is(":checked") &&
      localVar.userLocation ){

      localVar.image.img[totalImages] = localVar.userLocation;
      totalImages++;

      if( localVar.tmp%2!==0 && localVar.tmp>1){
        localVar.canvasHeight += localVar.userLocation.height;
        localVar.lastLoc = 1;
      }
```

```
      }
 // styling canvas
    myCanvas.width = 300;
    myCanvas.height = localVar.canvasHeight;
    //myCanvas.height = 700;
    myCanvas.style.background = "RGB(248,248,248)";
    var ctx = myCanvas.getContext('2d');
```

First of all, it hides the **Pick Fotos** button as we don't want the user to select images after they have clicked on the **Create Collage** button. Along with this button, it also hides the location switch. The canvas is now being displayed, and we augment the `localVar.image.img[]` array of images if the user selects the location to be viewed as an image in collage. Then, we set the properties of the canvas, the width is set to 300 (it might be set according to the screen size for a responsive design), and the height is set equal to `localVar.canvasHeight`, which contains the total height that is required for the canvas. After this, we set the initial values of certain variables that we will use during the whole process.

```
        var offsetX = 0;
        var offsetY = 0;
        var tmpHeight = 0;
        var firstColHeight = 0;
        var secondColHeight = 0;

        for( var i=0;i<totalImages;i++ ){

          var img = localVar.image.img[i];
          // to maintain aspect ratio of image.
          var ratio = (myCanvas.width/2) / img.width;
          var height = img.height * ratio;



          var tmp = i+1;

          if( tmp===1 ){
            offsetX = 0;
            offsetY = 0;
          }
          else if( tmp%2===0 && tmp>1 ){
            offsetX = myCanvas.width / 2;
          }
```

```
    else{
      offsetX = 0;
    }
     if( tmp%2===0 && tmp>2 ){
      ctx.drawImage(img, (offsetX+5), (secondColHeight+5),
        ((myCanvas.width/2)-10), (height-10) );


    }
    else if( tmp%2!==0 && tmp>2){

      if( localVar.lastLoc===1 && (img.src===localVar.userLocation.
 src) ){
          ctx.drawImage(img, (offsetX+5), (firstColHeight+5),
            ((myCanvas.width)-10), (height-10) );

      }
      else{
        ctx.drawImage(img, (offsetX+5), (firstColHeight+5),
          ((myCanvas.width/2)-10), (height-10) );

      }

    }
    else{

      ctx.drawImage(img, (offsetX+5), (offsetY+5),
        ((myCanvas.width/2)-10), (height-10))
    }


    if(tmp%2!==0){
      firstColHeight = height;
    }
    else{
      secondColHeight = height;

    }


  }
```

Next, the `for` loop starts and cycles through all the images that are selected by the user and stored in the `localVar.image.img[]` array, and draws each image on the canvas using the `ctx.drawImage()` function. This function requires five parameters (five in our case, otherwise it may vary). The first is the image object, the second and third are offsets in pixels for the top-left corner from which images will be drawn, the fourth and fifth are the custom width and height of the image about which the image will be spanned. The `ctx` is called context of the canvas.

```
$('#actionBtns').show();
$('#createCollage').hide();


$('#deleteCollage').on('click',function(event) {
  /* Act on the event */
  $('#imgDisplay').html('');
  $('#actionBtns').hide();
  localVar.imgCounter = 0;
  var myCanvas = document.getElementById('displayCanvas');
  var ctx = myCanvas.getContext('2d');
  ctx.clearRect(0, 0, myCanvas.width, myCanvas.height);
  $(myCanvas).hide();
  localVar.canvasHeight = 0;
  localVar.image.img = [];
  localVar.tmp = 1;
  $('#pickImage').show();
  $('.locationSwitch').show();
});

});
```

 A full description of other code fragments can be seen as comments in the JavaScript file.

Having drawn the collage, we should now attach events to the three buttons that are displayed at the bottom of the collage. These are the cloud saving button (through `imgur`), the download as `.png` file button, and the clear the current canvas and draw a new one button.

The **Delete** button clears the canvas, hides it, and then displays the **Pick Fotos** button again while it hides the three action buttons. It appears as if the app has reverted to its previous state and now the user has to, once again pick a different set of images for making collage.

The download as a `.png` file button is actually a link, and on clicking this link, it retrieves the data URL of the content of the canvas, and then sets the `href` attribute of this link to that URL and after setting the download attribute with the name of the image (we have used random string with the `fotofox_` prefix) that you want to download with, it makes the image download forcibly without following the link any further.

Finally, the **Share** button uploads your collage to an image-sharing site known as `http://imgur.com/`. The benefit of using `imgur` is that you can upload your image to it either by using its JS v3 API, or manually, and in return you get a link that points to this image. This link can be sent over e-mails and messages. So, instead of sending bulky images, the user can simply send the links.

Here is the code that demonstrates the usage of the `imgur` API:

```
$('#toImgur').on('click', function(){
    // this code snippet creates url of image in base64
      encoding

    var image = document.getElementById('displayCanvas').
      toDataURL('image/png', 0.9).split(',')[1];

    //imgur API
    $.ajax({

      url: 'https://api.imgur.com/3/image',
      type: 'post',
      headers: {
        Authorization: 'Client-ID c5efa529430990f'
      },
      data: {
        image: image
      },
      dataType: 'json',
      beforeSend:function(){

        $('#toImgur').html('<i class="fa fa-circle-o-notch fa-
          spin"></i>');
      },
      success: function(response) {

        if(response.success) {
          localVar.imgurLink = response.data.link;
          savelink();


        }
      },
      error:function( e ){
        $('#toImgur').html('<i class="fa fa-cloud"></i>')
        console.log('Error '+e.responseText);
      }

    });
```

Here, we again retrieve the URL of the content of the canvas by using the `toDataUrl()` function and send this data (as stored in the image variable) as a parameter of the request. In response to this request, we get a JSON back in which we get our required link inside `response.data.link`. After a successful response, the `savelink()` function is called which stores this link in the indexedDB. The code for the `savelink()` function is the same as the one that we used in the Check In! app to store the user's location and comments. Let's move towards the image-editing part.

```
// Edit image.
$("#pickImageForEdit").on('click',function(){

    // registering new mozActivity to pick image file
    var pickImageActivity = new MozActivity({
                                        name: "pick",
                                        data: {
                                                type: ["image/png",
                                                    "image/jpg",
                                                        "image/jpeg"]
                                        }
    });

    // if image successfully picked
    pickImageActivity.onsuccess = function() {

        $('#pickImageForEdit').html('New Foto');

        var myCanvas =
            document.getElementById("displayCanvasForEdit");

        // displays initially hidden canvas
        $(myCanvas).show();
        var ctx = myCanvas.getContext('2d');

        // styling canvas
        myCanvas.width = window.innerWidth - 30;
        myCanvas.style.background = "RGB(248,248,248)";
        ctx.clearRect(0, 0, myCanvas.width, myCanvas.height);

        var img = new Image();

        // loading image with picked up image
        img.src = window.URL.createObjectURL( this.result.blob );
```

Let's examine this code step by step. First of all, it registers the pick activity to pick an image from the user's gallery or camera; this code is the same as the one we wrote in order to pick images for a collage. Then, on successful retrieval of the image, the `onsuccess` function is fired, which displays the canvas element and sets its properties. After the creation of the canvas element, it creates the new image object and sets its `src` attribute to that which is returned after the image has been picked.

```
img.onload = function(){

    ctx.clearRect(0, 0, myCanvas.width, myCanvas.height);

    // maintaining aspect ratio
    var ratio = myCanvas.width / img.width;
    var height = img.height * ratio;

    myCanvas.height = height;

    ctx.drawImage(img, 5, 5, (myCanvas.width-10), (height-
        10));

    // displaying buttons
    $('#effectBtns').show();


    // attaching events to buttons inside image edit section.
    $('#grayEffect').click(function(){
        revert(img, height);
        grayscale(height);

    });
```

We have three more events that are attached to effects (sepia, invert, and revert). The code for the other events can be found in the JavaScript file.

```
pickImageActivity.onerror = function() {

    alert("unable to Pick Image");

};

});
```

After loading the image from its source, again a function is fired which draws the image on the canvas using the `ctx.drawImage()` function (where `ctx` is the context of the canvas). After drawing the image, it shows the set of effects buttons and binds the click event on these buttons with the appropriate functions, such as grayscale, sepia, and so on. After applying the effects, our major task is to upload the image to `imgur` or download the image. To perform these tasks, there are functions that have been earlier defined in order to download from and store in `imgur`, in the collage section. For any errors that may have occurred when the image was picked, there is already a function that handles the error, and displays an alert for that error.

Let's see how the grayscale function manipulates the pixel data of the canvas to give a grayscale effect to our image. Other functions such as sepia, blur, and invert, can be easily understood after you grasp the concept of pixel data manipulation.

For permanent changes to the canvas, we need to modify the pixel data of the canvas and then save the canvas with the modified data.

Here comes the grayscale function:

```
// grayscale effect
function grayscale(height){

    var myCanvas = document.getElementById('displayCanvasForEdit');
    var ctx = myCanvas.getContext('2d');

    var imageData = ctx.getImageData(5, 5, (myCanvas.width-10),
    (height-10) );
    var data = imageData.data;

    for(var i = 0; i < data.length; i += 4) {

        var r = data[i];  // red
        var g = data[i + 1]; // green
        var b = data[i + 2]; // blue

        // sets R,G,B to average value, this concept is used for Grayscale
    effect
        data[i] = data[i + 1] = data[i + 2] = (r+g+b)/3;
    }
    ctx.clearRect(0,0,myCanvas.width,myCanvas.height);
    // overwrite original image
    ctx.putImageData(imageData, 5, 5 );

    return true;
}
```

This function is used to change the image's effect to grayscale. What's actually happening here is, we are retrieving the image data using the ctx.getImageData() function, which accepts four parameters. The first and second are the top-left coordinates and the third and fourth ones are the width and height of the image. The data is stored in imagedata, data (here, we are retrieving the pixel data as an array). Next, we have a for loop that cycles through the length of this data and inside the for loop, the main concept is present. The value of red is stored in data[i], and similarly, the value of green and blue are stored in data[i+1] and data[i+2] respectively. Grayscale is basically an average value of R,G,B values, so we set the value of data[i], data[i+1], and data[i+2]b to (r+g+b) / 3. To draw the image with modified data, we use ctx.putImagedata(), which again accepts three parameters. The first one is the image data (modified one), and the other two are top-left offsets.

Here, we take the image's initial data and manipulate it according to our needs, and redraw the image on the canvas with this modified data:

That's all for our image-editing part. The last part is to view the previous images that are saved in imgur.

View previous functionality

Until now, we have seen how the collage is made, how an image can be edited with changes to its pixel data, and how to download the pictures or share them on cloud services like imgur. Since services like imgur return a link to where our image is stored, you will now learn how to add a functionality for viewing previous images and their imgur links, and how to share these links using e-mail or other third-party applications that are installed on the device.

Here's the code for that:

```
// function to view previously edited fotos
function viewPrevious(){

    // empty list
    $('.prevListings ul').html('');

    var objectStore = localVar.db.transaction("links").
objectStore("links");

    objectStore.openCursor().onsuccess = function(event) {

      var cursor = event.target.result;

      if (cursor) {


        $('.prevListings ul').append('<li class="list"><img
        class="img-thumbnail img-responsive" width="60"
        height="60" src="'+cursor.value.link+'"> <small><i
        class="fa fa-link"></i>
        '+(cursor.value.link)+'</small> <button class="btn
        btn-sm btn-action shareBtn"><i class="fa fa-share-
        alt"></i></button></li>');

        cursor.continue();



      }
    };
}
```

This function is called when the user clicks on the **Previous fotos** button on the main screen of our application. This function retrieves the content stored in `indexedDB` and displays it using `<li>` elements. This function is the same as the one we used in the Check In! app.

The explanation of the code is not necessary as it has already been explained in *Chapter 4, Diving Deeper with the Fox Creating Richer Apps.*

We successfully added a share functionality to our list of images so that one can easily share the link using e-mail or any other third-party application that is installed in the device for the same purpose.

Here's the code.

```
$(document).on('click','.shareBtn', function(){
    new MozActivity({
        name: "share",
        data: {
            number: 1,
            // imgut link of image that you want to share
            url: localVar.imgurLink
        }
    });

});
```

This code registers a new mozActivity share with data as required by the activity. This opens a pop-up window that asks you to select the app, and completes the requisite action.

Summary

In this chapter, you have learned about the various Web APIs and Web Activities. You have also learned how to apply them, with the help of code samples. You then applied your knowledge of Web APIs in order to build FoxFoto, which is an app that edits and shares images.

In the next chapter, you will learn to debug and test Firefox OS applications so that the applications that you build are optimized and run smoothly, even on devices with low processing power.

7
Testing Your Firefox OS Application

In this chapter, you will start off with basic **Quality Assurance (QA)** and unit testing. You will then learn to use Firefox developer tools to debug your app, use app validator to test applications, and use Spoof Firefox add-on for testing. You will also learn how to improve the performance of a Firefox OS application. We will go through the following topics in detail:

- Getting to know about QA and unit testing
- Using Firefox developer tools for debugging
- Using app validator to test applications
- Improving app's performance
- Using Spoof Firefox OS add-on

Introducing quality assurance

After building a few Firefox OS applications using various Web APIs, we have finally reached the point where we will have to test our application vigorously to ensure that the developed apps are robust and reliable. In this chapter, we will use some of the techniques that are used by programmers to develop their apps in a professional manner. It is a characteristic of every good programmer to thoroughly test their app to ensure the achievement of positive results in each and every possible practical situation. These techniques, at first glance, may seem boring, complex, or time consuming; however, to ignore or leave them for the future is not wise, as these tests will be of immense use to you when the codebase of your application grows.

The art of building apps and testing them during the development process itself is commonly known as **Test Driven Development** (TSD), and is extremely helpful in the process of building robust applications. This is the recommended development workflow that is required to build professional applications.

Unit testing

The first tool in our arsenal of QA is unit testing. Application testing has a colossal importance nowadays, as these applications run on multiple devices and platforms. So, it is very important to ensure that the apps delivers an outcome in any and every situation so that they do not lead to a bad user experience. Testing is a way of judging our application's performance in every practical situation. Unit testing refers to the testing of a particular unit or module of your code, one at a time.

There are several tools and frameworks available on the market for the same purpose. We will use QUnit, which is a very popular JavaScript Unit testing Framework.

 You can find the detailed documentation about QUnit at http://qunitjs.com/intro.

You are now ready with QUnit to write our first unit test for Clickr. First of all, take a look at this function (I have modified this slightly for the purpose of demonstrating unit testing):

```
function changeTimer( timeLeft ) {

  $(('#timer').text(( timeLeft - 1 ));
  return (timeLeft -1);

}
```

The `changeTimer` function takes the `timeLeft` argument and updates the text inside the element with the `timer` id, and returns the new value, which is decremented by 1 in place of the the previous value. For `Clickr`, this function plays the important role of decrementing the timer by 1 after every subsequent second passes. Now, let's test this function using QUnit.

The following is the HTML code for displaying the test results:

```
<!DOCTYPE html>
<html>
<head>
  <meta charset="utf-8">
  <title>QUnit Example</title>
  <link rel="stylesheet" href="http://code.jquery.com/qunit/qunit-
    1.18.0.css">
```

```
    </head>
    <body>
      <div id="qunit"></div>
      <div id="qunit-fixture"></div>
      <script src="https://code.jquery.com/jquery-
        1.11.3.min.js"></script>
      <script src="https://code.jquery.com/qunit/qunit-
        1.18.0.js"></script>
      <script src="script.js"></script>
      <script>
        QUnit.test("Check counter", function( assert ) {
            assert.equal( changeTimer(5), 4);
            assert.equal( changeTimer(3), 2);
            assert.equal( changeTimer(1), 0);
            assert.equal( changeTimer(0), undefined);
      });
      </script>
    </body>
    </html>
```

This small `html` file is the minimum requirement for QUnit to run the test and display the result successfully. We need to include QUnit's CSS and JS files. We have used the two `div` elements with `qunit` id and qunit-fixture respectively (these will be used to display the results in a beautified manner, as shown in the next screenshot). The `script.js` file contains the code for the `changeTimer` function, which tests. From this function, we expect to update the `#timer` element element to decrement the value of `timeLeft` by 1, until it becomes 0. As the value of `timeLeft` approaches 0, it prevents the function from updating it to the value of -1 and return `null`, as the timer cannot be negative in any case. Let's take a look at the results of QUnit in the following screenshot:

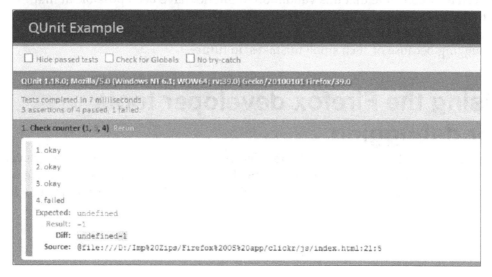

The result states that test number 4 fails while the other tests (1, 2, and 3) pass, which means that the function returned -1 when the value of timeLeft is set to 0. We did not expect this to happen, and it means that our function is not yet free of errors and requires some modifications. So, we will now put a validation check on our function for the '0' condition in order to get the expected result. The final function looks like this:

```
function changeTimer( timeLeft ) {
  // validation check at '0' value

              if( timeLeft === 0 ){

      clearInterval( clickr.timer );
    showResult();

  }else{

    $('#timer').text(( timeLeft - 1 ));
    return (timeLeft-1);

  }
  }
```

Now, we have put a validation check in our function to check the '0' condition. This check clears the interval of calling the function any further after the value of timeLeft approaches zero, and it also ensures that no value is returned when timeLeft approaches 0.

We can now conclude that this validation might not have been possible at first without unit testing our app. Unit testing is a powerful and useful technique that helps us to write flawless code and saves us the time that might get wasted in debugging because of such small mistakes, in future.

Using the Firefox developer tools for debugging

The Firefox developer tools are a handy, in-browser set of various tools that are very helpful in bringing the HTML, CSS, and JS of any page at your fingertips. While we debug our code, we need to obtain the details of a stylesheet, or check whether a JS file is loaded or not.

We can easily do this with the help of the Firefox developer tools. The toolkit contains numerous tools for a variety of purposes to help a developer with application development. Let's now discuss how to use some of these handy tools while we debug applications.

Console

Console is an in-browser logging zone where HTML, CSS, JS, and other errors are displayed. Not only the errors, but warnings and unexpected results. We have already discussed how you can open console for your Firefox OS application in *Chapter 2, Running Firefox OS Simulator with WebIDE*.

You must have already used console to log your result of JS code using the `console.log(message)` function, while some old-school JS programmers still prefer the use of `window.alert()` to log their messages. However, using alerts is quite annoying sometimes, and with the use of `console.log()`, you can silently log your results in console while testing, and take a look at them later on.

We also used console logging a few times in erroneous output of various functions in the Check In! application. We have used `console.log()` to log when there is an error in getting the user's current location, or inside the `initDB()` function when there is an error in connecting to `indexedDB`. The code snippets are as shown from `app.js` of Check In!:

```
function error(err) {
   console.warn('ERROR(' + err.code + '): ' + err.message);
}

request.onerror = function (e) {
   console.log("creation error:"+ e);
};
```

With the help of console, we can study the workflow of an application step by step to find the sources of errors in the execution of applications in different runs. We have made a new variant of the Check In! application, which has `console.log()` included in every major JavaScript function so that we can know which function is called when the user interacts with the application.

This workflow also proves to be useful while debugging for unexpected problems during the execution of the application, and it is helpful when we need to decide where to set breakpoints while testing or finding a bug.

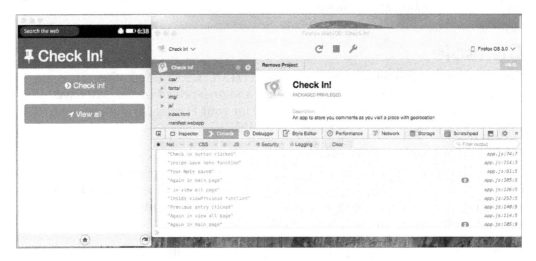

As you can see in the preceding screenshot, we interacted with the application just like a normal user would, and we opened the console via the WebIDE developer tools. First, we click on the **Check In!** button, and we get the message **Check in button clicked**. Then, we enter some comments about our current location and save the note, which gives us the **Inside save note function** message as well as the **Your note saved** message.

Now, we click on the **Back** button to go to the main page, and that gives us the **Again in main page** message. We may wish to see our previous notes, so we click on **View all** and this gives us the **in view all page** and **Inside viewPrevious function** message. Now, we click on the entry that we just recorded. This gives us the message **Previous entry clicked**. Now, we will get the same messages when we go back to the view all page and the main page respectively.

These messages help me as a debugger or a QA analyst, or you as a learner, to understand what exactly the application is doing at a given point in time, and let me know in which function I can find a bug when I perform a specific action in the application.

Some other important tools in developer toolkit are listed, as follows:

- **Inspector**: This tool helps us to examine the HTML structure of our app. It can be used to individually study the properties of any HTML elements parsed in that page.

- **Debugger**: This is an in-browser JavaScript debugger that can be used to debug the scripts loaded by the page. Whether it is to find breakpoints or to beautify our code, we can do all this right from our browser.

- **Style Editor**: This is a handy stylesheet editor. It can edit CSS of the page in runtime which enables us to see the changes live.

- **Performance**: This is used for performance profiling of web applications. It is used to profile JS function calls and monitor the performance of any app.

- **Network**: You can see all the external requests that your app makes during runtime, such as loading fonts from Google fonts, loading jQuery from its CDN, and so on. You can also see your AJAX calls in it. The type of request, such as GET or POST can also be seen in it. Basically, this tool helps us to cross-examine the external requests that your app/page made for its rendering. The following screenshot shows the network requests made by the Check In! application:

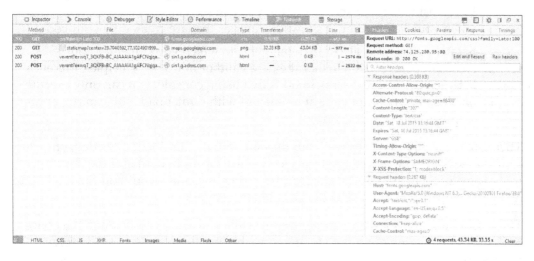

Here, you can see that there are a total of four requests that are being made by the Check In! application for it's rendering. The first one is Google fonts, the second is the image from Google Maps that contains the user's location, and so on.

For the first call to Google fonts we can see the Status code of 200 (the full list of status codes can be found at `http://www.w3.org/Protocols/rfc2616/rfc2616-sec10.html`) on the extreme left, which means the request has succeeded with no errors. Then, it is followed by the method of requests; in this case, it is `GET`, and for the bottom two, it is `POST`. Columns 4, 5, 6, 7, and 8 show the Domain to call, type of data, data transformed, size of data, and the time taken to complete that request respectively.

At the extreme right, we have the list of all the information, including browser headers (both response and request), parameters sent, cookies received, and timings of requests. From that panel we can gain full knowledge about what our application is doing, which external resource it is calling, from which domain, and so on.

So, here it is evident that the network analyzing tool is very useful when it comes to analyzing and examining your external requests and seeing their respective responses.

- **Storage**: This one is only important if you are using the localStorage API (HTML5) or indexedDB (as we used in Check In!) to store client data in the browser itself. It is disabled by default and one can enable it from **Settings** (by clicking on the gears icon) in the top-right corner of the developer tools. Here, inside the indexedDB section you can see your objectStore, and then when you click further, it shows the entries that are created by your code.

- **Scratchpad**: This is also a JS debugger into which you can enter your JS code snippets to test whether they are valid or not. The principle difference between console and scratchpad is that using console, you can only execute one line of JavaScript code at a time but with scratchpad, you can run entire snippets of JavaScript code.

There are some other tools as well, but they are initially disabled; if needed, one can enable them by clicking on the settings icon in the top-right corner of the developer tools, some of them are canvas, shader editor, timeline, and so on. You can read more about developer tools at the Mozilla Developer Network.

These developer tools are immensely useful while you are going through the phase of rigorous debugging of your code. If you wisely use these tools, it will surely reduce your time in debugging and increase your productivity as a developer.

Profiling performance by using the profiler

The **Performance** tool gives you an internal look at your app's responsiveness, JS performance, and function's calling order. This tool helps you to understand your application in terms of how your application's code is rendering in the browser, step-by-step from one function to another. Before we dive into further details, take a good look at the following screenshot:

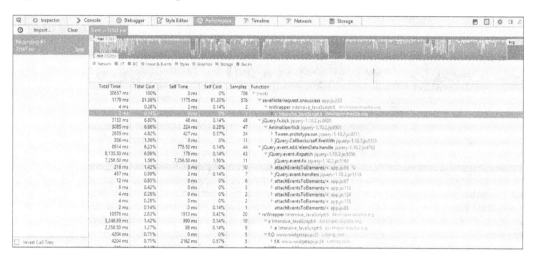

The information that is given in the preceding screenshot was generated by using performance profiling, which is Firefox's in-built tool. Here, we are checking the performance of the Check In! app. To generate this information for your own apps, you have to start recording by clicking on the clock icon in the top-left corner of the frame, and after clicking this, you can just start using your app normally for some time. Then, after some time, return to performance and stop profile recording again by clicking on the same icon. This process will generate the above type of table for your application.

Let's examine the preceding screenshot. This table is called the Call Tree, the bar-graph like panel just above call tree is called **Flame Chart**, and the panel at the top with a blue background is known as **Frame rate**. The following is a brief explanation of the various components of Performance.

Call tree

Call tree is the most intuitive of all. From call tree, we get the information about function calling and rendering. It stacks the code executing at the time of rendering.

The columns in call tree are as follows:

- **Samples** displays the numbers of samples of a function taken while we were executing that function.

- **Self cost** displays the same information in percentage of the aforementioned samples. The higher the self cost for any function, the higher the need for optimization for that function. This function is taking a long time to run, or is called very often, which means it is of the highest priority when it comes to optimization.

- **Self time** shows the time taken in executing the captured samples in milliseconds.

Under the function column we have a list of functions which are called during our recording period. They are nested and can be expanded by clicking the arrow. The function enlisted inside a function is called first, and then the containing function is called. For example, in the row we selected (in the screenshot), c is inside nrWrapper which means c is called first, and then the nrWrapper function, and the same goes on for all the enlisted functions.

One more thing that you may have noticed is that **intensive JavaScript** is written in front of these functions. It is due to the use of the alert() statement that we have used to display the success message after saving the user's note. It is called intensive as alert blocks JS main thread, and anything that hangs the JS main thread comes under intensive JavaScript, and therefore should be avoided. The JS file with which the function is associated can be found by clicking on the name of the file listed after the outermost function. In the preceding screenshot, the self cost of **saveNote/ request.onsuccess** is **81.30%**, which is the highest among all, which means that this function is in the utmost need of optimization among all other functions, for better performance of the application.

Flame chart

Flame chart also gives us valuable information about the JavaScript stack at every millisecond of execution. The x axis represents time and the y axis represents functions on the call stack. The color code makes it easy to distinguish between functions in the stack.

The higher and wider the stack, the more time it takes and the more complex the function executing in that period.

Frame rate

Frame rate is a measure of the app's responsiveness. A low frame rate can result in a lagging application. A frame rate of 60 fps is required for smooth performance of the app. In the case of web apps, it is the work that a browser does in order to repaint the screen. It is important when animations are present, which means that if there is a low frame rate, then the animations might appear sluggish or odd. Suppose when a browser moves over an element, and there is a change in the element state, then to update that state, the browser completes in that frame. Now, if an element needs a complex update, this can't be done with same frame rate (the frame rate lowers), and hence the browser may appear junky. The amount of work, regardless of how complex the updated is, must be broken up into blocks of ~16 ms maximum in order to guarantee 60 fps. If you can break a complex update into small pieces, where the amount of work is 16 ms pieces, you can do complex things at 60 fps.

Therefore, it is quite important to keep your frame rate up to 60 fps, to keep your application appearing smooth to the user.

Improving the app's performance

The performance of any application is vital for its success in the market. A user judges the quality of an application from its performance, whether it is the responsiveness, refreshing of frames (framerate), or memory usage (though indirectly perceived) of the app. All are important entities while determining any app's performance. Performance is one of the major factors for the application to compete with other apps of the same genres, and therefore, It needs to be critically tested and maximized.

There are numerous reasons for any app to exhibit a poor performance, some of which are summarized as follows:

* Non responsive design while using it on multiple platforms and devices
* The frame rate is not around 60Hz, which is best perceived by human eye
* Synchronous AJAX calls, mainly in web apps
* Loading of unnecessary CSS and JS files that are not needed in the first place for a page
* Extensive use of memory consuming things, such as WebGL, 2D and 3D canvas, and so on, for animations

The app which will be responsive in any device will be fantastic in terms of user experience. The app must be responsive and adaptive to any device, and it should be made to run to enrich the user experience.

Another major mistake that most of the developers make is making synchronous calls in JS, which is considered bad practice. Synchronous calls hang the browser until their response is received, whereas asynchronous calls use the callback method and run in parallel. When an asynchronous call runs, the other parts of the code also execute. Therefore, making asynchronous calls reduces a significant amount of loading time, and is also very essential in developing superfast, non-blocking applications.

The next issue is to load unnecessary CSS and JS files that are not needed in the first place for a particular page. It is recommended that they should be loaded only when it is necessary for them to load, this can also speed up apps loading time. It is now becoming a common practice to include minified or compressed (whitespaces removed) CSS and JS files for faster loading. You can also consider using defer and `async` attributes with the script tag. The `async` attribute indicates that the browser should, if possible, execute the script where the Boolean attribute has been used asynchronously. One important thing to note is that it has no effect on inline scripts, which are scripts that do not have an `src` attribute. The `defer` attribute is a `Boolean` attribute that is set to indicate to a browser that the script where this attribute has been used is meant to be executed after the document has been parsed.

 Please note that this feature has not yet been implemented by all the browsers.

Another reason that reduces performance in many applications is the use of JS for animations to increase the interactivity of apps. This is done by using third-party plugins like WebGL, `animation.js`, and so on. Instead of using JS, one can use CSS based animations and transitions to reduce the load on apps and indirectly save some memory and hence increasing the performance in some way.

Hence, with the help of the aforementioned minute techniques, you can increase your app's performance by a reasonable amount.

Using the App Validator

According to Mozilla, App Validator is a tool that is built to test those apps that are ready for submission to Firefox Marketplace. Apps submitted to Marketplace are automatically tested using App Validator, which is the first step of the reviewing process.

App Validator checks various points, like syntax of the manifest file, whether the `launch_path` exists or not, if there are there any CSP violations, or if the app contains any JS syntax errors. There are various other things that App Validator checks to ensure the security of both the app and the user.

 App Validator is available both online at `https://marketplace.firefox.com/developers/validator` and offline at `https://github.com/mozilla/app-validator`.

To use the App Validator offline, first install it using the setup instructions that are provided, and after installing the validator, open **Terminal** (MAC or Linux users), or command prompt (Windows users), and type the following code:

```
app-validator /path/to/your/manifest -v
```

The second argument v is used here to display a verbose summary of results returned by App Validator. The complete list of arguments can be found at the links provided in the preceding information box.

You can have it installed on your computer so that you can build your app according to the guidelines provided by Mozilla by validating your app using App Validator before you submit it to Marketplace. It will help you in detecting all the various CSP violations (errors and warning) that occur in your application.

Spoof Firefox OS Add-on

If you own an Android device and don't want to test your FxOS app on a real Firefox device, then a good news for a developer like you is that you can now test your FxOS apps right on your Android device. This is possible by installing the Spoof FxOS add-on to the Firefox browser of your Android device. This can be downloaded from `https://addons.mozilla.org/en-US/android/addon/spoof-fxos/`.

What the Spoof FxOS add-on does?

According to Mozilla, this add-on makes Firefox on Android send the Firefox OS User-Agent, and disables Flash, to make it simpler to test on Android how a site is likely to work on Firefox OS. A full emulation is not possible, especially for video and performance issues.

This means that the Firefox browser in your Android device will just pretend to be the Firefox OS browser, which enables you to test and debug your Firefox OS apps on your Android device. After downloading the add-on, enable the add-on from the browser's settings by clicking on the **Enable Spoofing as Firefox OS** checkbox, and simply reload the app to see the changes.

Summary

In this chapter, you learned about unit testing your Firefox OS application with the help of QUnit and debugging your application with the help of Firefox's Developer Tools. You studied some of the important tools in depth along with references to the various applications developed in the book. You also learned how to improve application performance, use application validator, and use the Spoof Firefox OS add-on.

In the next chapter, you will learn how to submit your applications to Firefox Marketplace and update applications on the marketplace. You will also study the various review criteria used by Marketplace to review the applications. Finally, you will learn how to publish paid applications to Marketplace, and port existing web applications to Firefox OS.

Firefox Marketplace – Setting up Your Bazaar

8

In this chapter, you will get to know about Firefox Marketplace, and learn how to submit and update applications on Marketplace. You will also study the various review criteria used by Marketplace to review applications. You will then learn how to publish paid applications to Marketplace, and port existing Web applications to Firefox OS. We will go through the following topics in detail:

- Getting to know about Firefox Marketplace
- Submitting your application to Firefox Marketplace
- Updating your application in Marketplace
- Going through Marketplace review criteria
- Publishing paid applications to Marketplace
- Porting existing web app to Firefox OS

Firefox Marketplace

Firefox Marketplace (`http://marketplace.firefox.com`) is an online marketplace that offers you free and paid applications for Firefox on Android, Desktop, and Firefox OS. Let's take a look at a screenshot of the Firefox Marketplace:

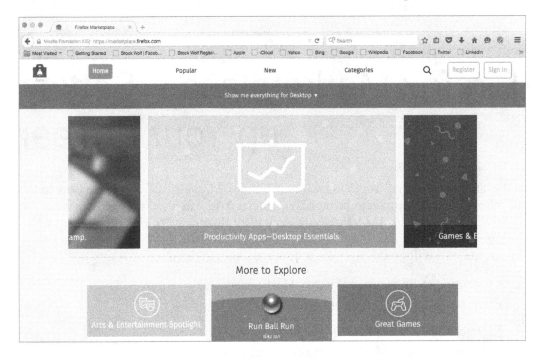

Just like any other other applications store, such as Apple App Store or Google Play Store, Firefox Marketplace offers you a wide range of applications from games to productivity applications. Firefox Marketplace has been set up in a manner that allows developers to submit their applications in a very easy way. Although it is the main channel for the distribution of Firefox OS applications, you are not compulsorily required to use it. The review criteria of Marketplace are also very well documented and you will study the review guidelines for application submission as well, later in this chapter.

First of all, we will submit our application Clickr to Marketplace as a packaged application and demonstrate the steps taken while submitting the application to Marketplace with appropriate screenshots.

Submitting your application to Firefox Marketplace

There are certain things that you need to keep in mind when you consider submitting an application to Marketplace. If you wish to submit your application as a hosted application, then you need to make sure that the MIME type of the manifest file is served correctly (they should be be served with this `Content-Type` header of `application/x-web-app-manifest+json`). However, if you wish to submit your application as a packaged application, then you will need to compress the application in the `.zip` format.

One common mistake that people make is that they zip the folder which contains the source code of their application. Don't make that mistake, or else your application won't pass the validation test. Remember, the manifest file should be at the root level of your zipped file.

Let's submit our application now. First of all, let's compress our application; users of OS X can do so by selecting all the files and folders, and right-clicking to select **Compress 6 items**. This will create a file called `Archive.zip` for you. Let's rename it to `Clickr.zip`.

Open `https://marketplace.firefox.com/` and click on the **Register** button on the top-right side of the web page. This will ask for details such as your e-mail ID, password, and date of birth. Fill in the details and click on the **Sign Up** button. This will show you a message that asks you to confirm your e-mail ID, and will also notify you that a verification link has been sent to your e-mail ID. When you click on the link that you have received in your inbox, you will get the message: **You are now ready to use Firefox Marketplace**. Now, you can sign in to your account using your login credentials.

Go to `https://marketplace.firefox.com/developers/` and click on the button that says: **Submit your app to the marketplace**.

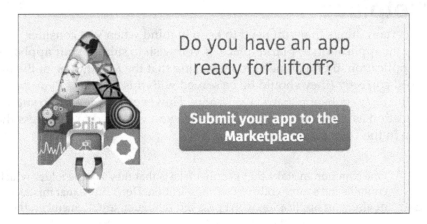

 You can also do so by directly visiting this link: `https://marketplace.firefox.com/developers/submit/terms`.

Now, you will see a screen that displays **Developer Agreement**. Here, click on **Agree and continue**. This will take you to the **Submit an app** screen. You will be asked to select the type of your application, whether it is designed for Firefox OS, Firefox for Desktop, Firefox Mobile, or Firefox Tablet. Select **Firefox OS**, and you will get two options: **Hosted App** and **Packaged App**. Select **Packaged App** and upload the `Clickr.zip` file.

The Marketplace will then will upload and validate your application, and ask for **App Minimum Requirements**. You will have to check the boxes of the features that your app requires to function properly. This will ensure that your app stays hidden from users whose devices don't support the app. We don't have any such requirements, so just click on the **Continue** button.

This will now bring you to a page where you can edit details of the application, such as the description, add keywords, add categories, enter the privacy policy, and many other details. You will need to either enter a website URL for your application or an e-mail ID that will be publicly viewable. Also, you have will need to enter at least one screenshot for your application. I went ahead and added two for Clickr and submitted the form. Then, Marketplace asked me for **Content Ratings**. To obtain a content rating is quite simple, just click on the option for this on the left panel and it will take you to `https://www.globalratings.com/`, where you will have to fill up a form to get content ratings for your application. The global rating tool then issues an official Certification Letter as shown in the following illustration:

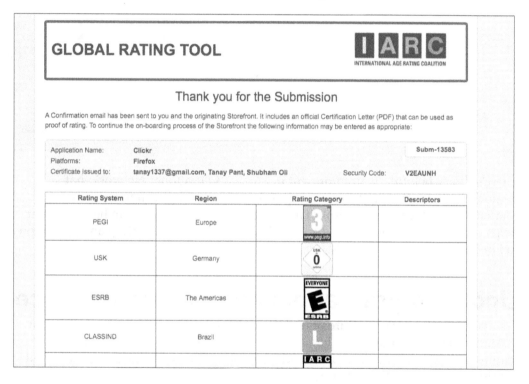

Once you are finished with this, your application will be automatically submitted for review to Marketplace reviewers. Once it has been reviewed, it will be publicly listed.

There's a very helpful diagram present in Mozilla's Developer Network that demonstrates the procedure involved in submitting an application to Firefox Marketplace in the form of a flowchart. I have attached this diagram here so that it helps you to understand the whole workflow involved in submitting an application to Firefox Marketplace correctly.

Updating your application in Marketplace

Let's now discuss the procedure of updating an application that is already present in Marketplace. You might need to update your applications frequently for either feature additions or bug fixes. The procedure for updating applications is different for Hosted Apps and Packaged Apps.

If you wish to make changes to a hosted application, then you simply need to update the source files on your web server and the changes will be pushed to the users. However, if there are major changes that need to be made to the manifest file on your server (for example, a change in the manifest's content or location), the application will be flagged for review again.

The procedure for packaged applications is slightly different. You will need to upload the archived package again, which will be flagged for review by Marketplace. Your application will be visible in Marketplace while the new version awaits review. Once the updated application has been reviewed, the users of your application will get a notification to update your application. Firefox OS in the user's device checks for app updates daily and notifies users about the same.

To update your application in Marketplace, click on **My Submissions**. Under **Manage My Submissions** click on **Status & Versions** for the application that you wish to update. Click on **Select a File** under **Upload New Version**. Quite easy, isn't it? Firefox Marketplace has this easy workflow for developers publishing applications, which is just the icing on the cake. The following illustration showing option to upload new version for an application in the Marketplace:

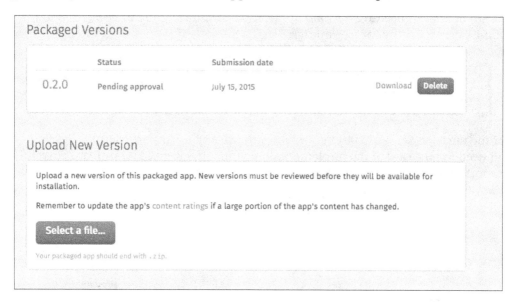

Marketplace review criteria

Let's now discuss the various criteria based on which the reviewers decide whether an application should be published in the Marketplace or not. One important thing to keep in mind is that Marketplace reviewers do not review an application on the basis of how it looks, but rather on the basis of the working of an application. The review process is quite fair and transparent, since Firefox Marketplace has reviewers from Mozilla's huge volunteer base as well, in addition to full-time employees.

Some of the main points that are considered while reviewing the application are: usability (navigation and functionality), security (take care of CSP guidelines), content (non-offensive and IARC rated), functionality, and the privacy policy of the application.

If your application adheres to these simple guidelines, and you follow all the instructions present in the previous chapters carefully, then you should not face any problem in your application being accepted in Marketplace.

Publishing paid applications in Marketplace

The submission procedure for paid applications differs slightly as compared to the submission procedure for free applications.

> Note that we are referring to paid applications on the Marketplace and not in-app payments (however, the submission procedure for both paid apps and in-app payment apps is the same).

For the purpose of in-app payments, you can use any third-party service but you will need to take care of the implementation yourself. Firefox Marketplace currently supports only Bango as their payment provider. The following illustration for submitting a paid application:

Now, while submitting paid apps to the marketplace, you will need to select the **Paid / In-app** tab instead of the **Free** tab. The rest of the procedure is pretty much the same. You just need to fill out the Compatibility and Payments section as well for Bango.

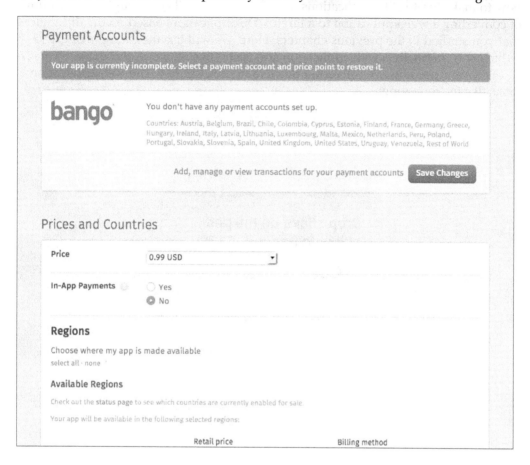

Remember, you will need to set up a payment account with Bango first. Firefox Marketplace also offers an option to promote the application in question as an upgrade to a free version. This option is present at the bottom of the page shown in the preceding screenshot. From here, you can select the application that you want to upgrade to the paid version. A drop-down shows you the list of applications submitted by you. Link the selected app through this option and your premium app will be promoted next to the free version.

Porting existing web apps to Firefox OS

Now, you will be study how to port existing web applications to Firefox OS; that is, how to make Firefox OS applications out of them. We will go through the workflow of converting a web application to a Firefox OS application, based on the differences that you studied in the previous chapters. Here, we will use the example of Clickr (which was originally a web application and is still live at `http://stockwolf.net/clickr/`) and see how we converted this to a Firefox OS app. The web application looks like the following:

Conversion of a web app to a hosted Firefox OS application

To convert a regular web application (without making any code changes) such as Clickr, we need to add an application manifest file to the root of the application that specifies details about the application. In addition to this, we need to add assets such as icons for the operating system to display them after the application has been installed.

However, these things get complicated if we have an application that intends to use privileged features to enhance the web application. In that case, we also need to take care of implementing such features in the Firefox OS version of the web application to use the appropriate WebAPIs. Also, the type of the application will then be changed from web to privileged, and all the permissions for the privileged WebAPIs will need to be specified in the manifest file. The following flowchart shows the basic workflow to convert a web application to a Firefox OS application.

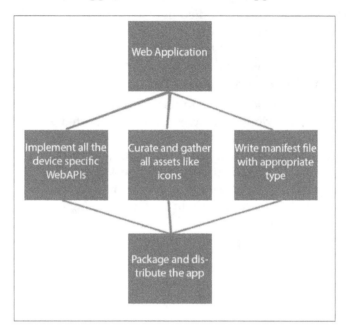

So, the workflow can be summarized into the following steps:

1. Take the web application that you wish to port into a Firefox OS application. This application can be built using the development toolkit of your choice. You can make use of angular, ember, jQuery, and so on. Just make sure that the framework that you are employing in the web application does not violate any CSP norms for Firefox OS applications.

2. Analyze the application, and see if you wish to implement any device-specific WebAPIs. If your web application is a camera app, then it would make sense to employ the Camera API to employ capturing a photo. Take a look at the complete list of WebAPIs on the Mozilla Developer Network. Choose the device APIs that you feel will have a positive impact on users and help your application to interact with them in a more personalized manner.

3. Curate and gather all assets such as images, icons, and CSS files so that the source code can be together and when you load assets from a remote web server, it will violate the CSPs. You will need to add icons for your applications as well. Make sure to include the appropriate icon sizes such as 60 pixels as a compulsion, otherwise Marketplace will not accept your application to submit your app.

4. Now, prepare the manifest file for your application. In the previous chapter, you have already studied how to prepare the manifest file for your applications. Make sure to include all the required details in there. Make sure that the type of the application is correct in the manifest file and the permissions for all the privileged WebAPIs that you have made use of in the application have been requested in the manifest file.

5. Now, it's time to package the application into a zipped file and submit it to Marketplace for review. You have successfully ported your application from a web application to Firefox OS. If your application is not of the privileged type, then you can also distribute your application as a hosted application in Marketplace, or even distribute it outside Marketplace. To self-publish a hosted application, you need to add an **Install** button to the application, which you already learned to do in *Chapter 4, Diving Deeper with the Fox Creating Richer Apps*.

This was the workflow that we followed in order to convert the web application to a Firefox OS Application. However, we also did an overhaul of the UI of the application for demonstration purposes. You should also try to port some of your amazing web applications to Firefox OS to get a clearer hang of this workflow.

Summary

In this chapter, you learned about Firefox Marketplace and submitted your first application to it. You then learned how to update a previously submitted application in Marketplace, review the criteria for the application in Marketplace, publish paid applications to Marketplace, and port existing web applications to Firefox OS. Finally, you studied the general workflow to be followed to convert any functional web application to a Firefox OS application.

In the next chapter, you will study how to maintain your Firefox OS code professionally. You will learn how to set up an account at GitHub, version-control an application, upload a local repository to GitHub, set up Travis CI for your repository, and host apps on RHCloud via git.

9
Maintaining Your Firefox OS Application Code Professionally

In this chapter, you will study how to maintain the source code of your application, professionally, using a distributed version control system such as Git. You might already make use of Git for version controlling, so we will just refresh our memories a bit on this topic by explaining the essentials. You will also how to host your project in a remote cloud repository such as GitHub and make your code open source so that other developers can also contribute to your Firefox OS application. You will also observe how you can deploy continuous integration systems such as Travis CI to take care of automated tasks, such as tests, with each change in the repository. Lastly, you will learn how to deploy hosted applications to RHCloud with the help of Git. We will go through the following topics in detail:

- Setting up an account at GitHub
- Version controlling your application
- Uploading your local repository to GitHub
- Setting up Travis CI for your repository
- Hosting apps on RHCloud via Git

Setting up an account at GitHub

So, let's get started with the task of setting up an account at GitHub. GitHub is a web-based repository hosting web service that allows users to version control their source code online. GitHub offers both private as well as public repositories. With the help of GitHub, other users can also discover your open source projects and contribute code to them. Isn't this the perfect place for your Firefox OS application's code to reside?

Go to `https://github.com/` and click on **Sign Up**. You will be asked for details, such as your name, e-mail ID, and a password. Then you will be asked for your account plan. Select the free one and you are good to go. Signing up at GitHub is as easy as setting up a developer account at Firefox Marketplace.

On the top-right corner of your screen, you have an option from where you can see your profile and your repositories as well as the repositories that you have contributed to. That's it, congratulations, you just set up your developer account at GitHub!

Version controlling your application

Let's now learn how we can version control our Firefox OS application for backup, where we store different versions, and collaboration. First of all, you will require Git on your system. You can download Git from Git's official website: `http://git-scm.com`. Simply download the application, and it will set up both the graphic-based and the command line-based Git for you. Let's continue our work further through the command line. I will go through the bare essentials of Git that are required to upload our source code to GitHub so that we don't have any difficulty deploying the application to RHCloud via Git. If you want an in-depth tutorial of Git, you need to take a look at the official documentation on their website, it is really very good.

So, I hope you have Git installed and working by now. You can go to the command line and type the following command to check if it's installed correctly:

```
git -version
```

If you get the version number as the output, then you are ready to go.

 You can take a look at the official documentation for troubleshooting Git installation at `http://git-scm.com/docs/user-manual.html` in a box for Git user manual.

Now I have my code, named `clickr - Gaia`, saved in a folder on the desktop. I will change my directory to get there. Then I will initialize an empty Git repository in the folder with the help of the following command (this command is executed at the command line in a terminal window, and you need to change to the root directory of the source code folder before you enter the command):

```
git init
```

I will take a look at the status of my Git repository by entering the status command `git status`. This will show me the list of untracked files in the Git repository. There are four types of files: untracked, staged, committed, and modified. The terminal looks like the following illustration:

```
Last login: Wed Jul 15 17:19:29 on ttys000
Tanays-MacBook-Air:~ tanay$ git --version
git version 2.3.2 (Apple Git-55)
Tanays-MacBook-Air:~ tanay$ cd Desktop/clickr\ -\ Gaia/
Tanays-MacBook-Air:clickr - Gaia tanay$ git init
Initialized empty Git repository in /Users/tanay/Desktop/clickr - Gaia/.git/
Tanays-MacBook-Air:clickr - Gaia tanay$ git status
On branch master

Initial commit

Untracked files:
  (use "git add <file>..." to include in what will be committed)

        .DS_Store
        css/
        fonts/
        img/
        index.html
        js/
        manifest.webapp

nothing added to commit but untracked files present (use "git add" to track)
Tanays-MacBook-Air:clickr - Gaia tanay$
```

Untracked means that these files reside in the folder but haven't been added to the repository. Adding an untracked file adds it to the staging area. Files in the staging area can be committed to the Git repository. Once a change to committed file is made, it becomes modified. After that, the file in question has to be added again to be committed. I will now enter the `git add —all` command to add all the files to the staging area. Now, when I enter `git status`, it will show me all the changes that need to be committed. Now that we have all the files ready to be committed, we can give the following command to commit the changes:

```
git commit -m "Initial Commit"
```

This gives me the following successful output in my console:

```
19 files changed, 1561 insertions(+)
    create mode 100755 css/bootstrap.min.css
 create mode 100755 css/buttons.css
 create mode 100755 css/font-awesome.min.css
 create mode 100755 css/headers.css
 create mode 100755 css/style.css
 create mode 100755 fonts/FontAwesome.otf
 create mode 100755 fonts/fontawesome-webfont.eot
 create mode 100755 fonts/fontawesome-webfont.svg
 create mode 100755 fonts/fontawesome-webfont.ttf
 create mode 100755 fonts/fontawesome-webfont.woff
 create mode 100755 img/icons/icon_128.png
 create mode 100755 img/icons/icon_16.png
 create mode 100755 img/icons/icon_48.png
 create mode 100755 img/icons/icon_60.png
 create mode 100755 index.html
 create mode 100755 js/bootstrap.min.js
 create mode 100755 js/clickr.js
 create mode 100755 js/jquery-1.11.3.min.js
 create mode 100755 manifest.webapp
```

Git has successfully committed all the files. The phrase in the double quotes in the following message was the commit message. You can see the commit messages for your previous commits by entering the command `git log`: My terminal's output looks like the following illustration:

```
● ● ●                 clickr - Gaia — bash — 80×24
Tanays-MacBook-Air:clickr - Gaia tanay$ git log
commit cb09ff2e7d85389a67772d537a93fecf69668c7a
Author: Tanay Pant <tanay@Tanays-MacBook-Air.local>
Date:   Thu Jul 16 18:27:43 2015 +0530

    Inital Commit
Tanays-MacBook-Air:clickr - Gaia tanay$
```

Congratulations, you have just version-controlled your Firefox OS application.

 Note that version tracking is now only on the local machine and nothing at all has been sent to GitHub. So, if you delete the folder, all your code and changes will be lost.

Now you can upload the repository to GitHub so that other developers can also contribute to the project. To do this, go to GitHub and enter the **+** icon on the top-right corner on the screen and click on **New repository**. Doing so will create a new repository for you and it will show you the instructions to upload your repository to GitHub, as shown in the screen below:

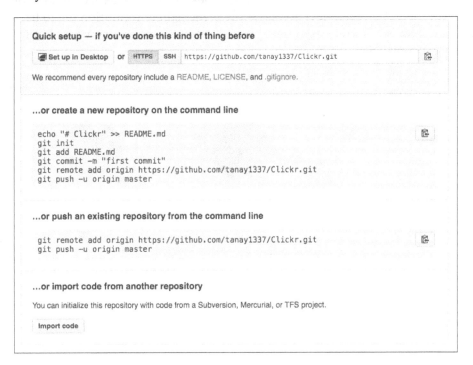

Since we have an existing repository, we enter the Git remote command that adds the online GitHub repository as the remote repository of our local repository. Then, we enter the push command, which will push our local repository upstream to GitHub. It will ask for your GitHub username and password while doing so.

Now, your repository will be live on GitHub for other developers or team members to contribute to. For greater details such as forking a GitHub repository and making pull requests to a team member's repository, you should refer to the official documentation of GitHub (`https://github.com/`) as it is beyond the scope of this book.

So, congratulations, you have just made your first version-controlled Firefox OS application live on GitHub. Now, it's time to learn how to integrate your GitHub accounts with a service such as Travis CI so that it can help you to automate some housekeeping tasks for our repository. You can sign up for a developer account at `https://travis-ci.org/`. It asks you to log in via your GitHub account, there you can go to your profile to view all your repositories to enable Travis CI builds for any one of them. You then have to add a `.travis.yml` configuration file to trigger automated Travis CI builds from next push. The workflow is documented in the following screenshot:

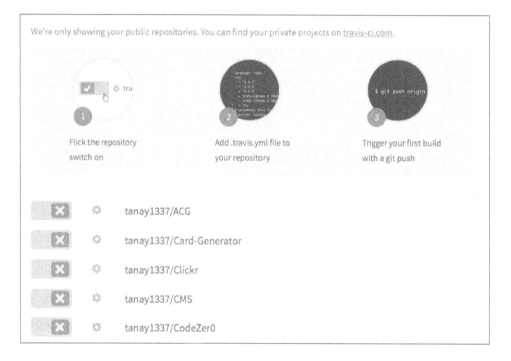

 You can find detailed platform-specific instructions for PHP and JavaScript at `http://docs.travis-ci.com`.

Hosting apps on RHCloud via Git

Let's now learn to deploy our installable and offline application to the cloud with the help of Git. We will use Red Hat's OpenShift to deploy our Firefox OS application. Go to https://www.openshift.com and sign up for a free account. You will be asked to write a domain name there; you can write anything you like. After signing up, click on **Add Application**. From there, you can select **PHP 5.4**. It will ask you for a public URL, which you can fill in. You can leave rest of the details as it is and click on **Create Application**. Doing so will bring up a set of instructions on your screen. Now, instead of continuing with the next steps from my machine, I will showcase how to continue with the help of a cloud-based development environment. We will use Cloud 9 IDE for this purpose. Simply go to https://c9.io and register there. Click on **Create a new Workspace**, select **Custom workspace,** and give it a name.

We are making use of the online development environment to save you the trouble of installing developer tools such as Git or Ruby on your machine, if you haven't done that already. My workspace now looks like the next screenshot.

Now you should go to the terminal and enter the following command to install RHC tools:

```
sudo gem install rhc
```

After the ruby gem for RHC tools is successfully installed, you should run the following command:

```
rhc setup
```

This screen will ask you for your OpenShift account details to set up or configure the toolkit. Now you should go back to the details screen of your OpenShift application, where it showed details to clone your application. When I did this, it gave me instructions to enter the following command:

```
git clone ssh://55a4a9d14382ec37ea000066@clickr-
tanaypant.rhcloud.com/~/git/clickr.git/
```

This successfully cloned the application onto my development environment. We can upload the whole source code of the application onto the directory that was cloned from OpenShift. Now, to add all the files to the server, we first need to add all the files to the VCS, commit them, and push them onto the server. This can be done by the following commands. Here's my console output:

```
tanay1337@clickr:~/workspace/clickr (master) $ git add --all

tanay1337@clickr:~/workspace/clickr (master) $ git commit -m "Initial
Commit"

[master 05b0cc5] Initial Commit

 13 files changed, 316 insertions(+), 274 deletions(-)

 create mode 100644 css/bootstrap.min.css

 create mode 100644 css/style.css

 create mode 100644 img/icons/icon_128.png

 create mode 100644 img/icons/icon_16.png

 create mode 100644 img/icons/icon_48.png

 create mode 100644 img/icons/icon_64.png

 create mode 100644 index.html

 delete mode 100644 index.php

 create mode 100644 js/bootstrap.min.js

 create mode 100644 js/clickr.js

 create mode 100644 js/jquery-1.11.3.min.js

 create mode 100644 manifest.appcache

 create mode 100644 manifest.webapp

tanay1337@clickr:~/workspace/clickr (master) $ git push

Counting objects: 19, done.
```

```
Delta compression using up to 8 threads.
Compressing objects: 100% (17/17), done.
Writing objects: 100% (18/18), 74.14 KiB | 0 bytes/s, done.
Total 18 (delta 0), reused 0 (delta 0)
remote: Stopping PHP 5.4 cartridge (Apache+mod_php)
remote: Waiting for stop to finish
remote: Waiting for stop to finish
remote: Building git ref 'master', commit 05b0cc5
remote: Checking .openshift/pear.txt for PEAR dependency...
remote: Preparing build for deployment
remote: Deployment id is 66979788
remote: Activating deployment
remote: Starting PHP 5.4 cartridge (Apache+mod_php)
remote: Application directory "/" selected as DocumentRoot
remote: -----------------------
remote: Git Post-Receive Result: success
remote: Activation status: success
remote: Deployment completed with status: success
To ssh://55a4a9d14382ec37ea000066@clickr-tanaypant.rhcloud.com/~/git/
clickr.git/
   bf275e5..05b0cc5  master -> master
```

As you can see in the following screenshot, the application is now live! I have opened the application in Safari: since the application senses that it is not being accessed via a Firefox OS device, it does not show us the **Install** button. As we have seen before, the application also does not show the Install button in a web browser in Firefox OS, if the application has already been installed in the device. You can carry out the same workflow in your personal system, if you have Ruby, RubyGems, and Git install. You are not required to go through C9 to carry out the process of deploying your application to OpenShift if you don't want to.

You can do the same process from your own machine.

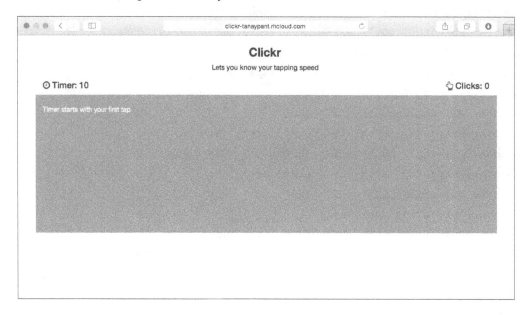

Congratulations, you have deployed your first Firefox OS application with the help of a Version Control System. As you will notice, your application will be set up by now on the URL that you were given while creating the application. Now you should fire up the Firefox OS Simulator and enter that URL in the browser. You will notice that the application with the **Install** button is present there. This application works offline too, as you might have noticed since we have included AppCache before.

Summary

In this chapter, you have learned how to set up an account at GitHub, version control the source code of your Firefox OS applications, and take your version controlled repository online with GitHub. Finally, you learned how to deploy Travis CI for your GitHub repository, and host Firefox OS applications on RHCloud via Git.

I hope you had a great time learning how to develop applications for Firefox OS. Don't just stop here, you have learned how to walk, now it's up to you how fast you can run. Go ahead and explore more about developing applications for Firefox OS, and develop some truly amazing applications. Make sure you share with us on social media the applications that you have built. *Stay hungry, stay foolish!*

Index

F

Firefox developer tools
  console 109-112
  debugger 111
  inspector 111
  network 111
  performance 111
  performance, profiling with profiler 113
  scratchpad 112
  storage 112
  Style Editor 111
  used, for debugging 108
Firefox Marketplace
  about 120
  application, submitting to 121-124
  application, updating 124, 125
  content rating, URL 123
  existing web apps, porting to 128
  paid applications, publishing 126, 127
  review criteria 125, 126
  URL 120-122
Firefox OS
  about 1
  applications, developing for 2, 3
  applications, uninstalling 20, 21
  architecture 3
  components, working 5
  devices 8, 9
  security model 6, 7
  URL 9, 11
Firefox OS applications
  about 24
  hosted applications 25
  manifest file, building 28
  packaged applications 25
  running, as hosted application 37-39
  running, on simulator 34, 36
  security access levels 27
  source code download, URL 35
  web app, converting to 128-130
Firefox OS color palette
  style guide, URL 70
Flame Chart 113, 114
Foundation
  URL 68

FoxFoto
  building 84
  HTML file 85
  previous images, viewing by adding
      functionality 101-103
  underlying JavaScript code 86-101
frame rate 115

G

Gaia
  URL 20
Gaia Building Blocks
  about 68, 70
  URL 68
Gaia, Firefox OS 4
Gecko, Firefox OS 4
Git
  apps, hosting on RHCloud via 137
  troubleshooting, URL 132
  URL, for download 132
GitHub
  account, setting up 132
  URL 132, 136
Gonk, Firefox OS 4

H

hosted applications
  about 25
  Firefox OS applications, running as 37-39
  making, installable 42-46
HTML5
  and open web applications 6

I

icons
  URL 30
initDB() function 55
installations
  WebIDE 11-14
install() function 42

M

manifest file, Firefox OS applications
about 28
application logic, constructing 32-34
building 28
directory structure 29
index file, constructing 30
stylesheet, constructing 32
Materialize
URL 68
Mozilla Developer Network
URL 29

N

new apps
creating, with WebIDE 14-17
installing, with WebIDE 14-17

O

OpenShift
URL 137
open web applications
and HTML5 6

P

paid applications
publishing, at Firefox Marketplace 126, 127
profiler
call tree 114
Flame chart 114
frame rate 115
used, for profiling performance 113

Q

Quality Assurance (QA)
about 105
unit testing 106-108
QUnit
URL 106

R

responsive design view
used, for checking responsiveness 72
RHCloud
apps, hosting via Git 137-140
runtime applications
browsing 19

S

SDK 2
security access levels
about 27
hosted apps 27
Internal/Certified apps 27
privileged apps 27
security model, Firefox OS 6, 7
simulator
Firefox OS applications, running 34, 36
Spoof FxOS add-on
about 118
URL 118
Stack Edit 6
startup time 25
status code definitions
URL 112
Stock Wolf
URL 128

T

Test Driven Development (TSD) 106
Travis CI
URL 136

U

UI blunders
avoiding 67, 68

V

viewPrevious() function 61

W

web activities
about 82-84
URL 84
web activities, for Firefox OS
browse 83
configure 83
dial 83
new 83
open 83
pick 83
record 83
save-bookmark 83
share 84
update 84
view 84
web and privileged APIs
about 76
alarm API 79
ambient light sensor API 77
apps API 80
battery Status API 77
browser API (Privileged) 81
contacts API 79
device orientation API 78
device Storage API (Privileged) 79
File Handle API 78
geolocation API 78
indexedDB 79
network information API 76
pointer lock API 78
proximity API 78
screen orientation API 78
simple PUSH API 80
TCP socket API (Privileged) 77
vibration API 78
web activities API 80
Web FM API 78
web notifications API 80
WebPayment API 80

Web APIs
about 76
certified APIs 81
certified level 76
privileged level 76
web and privileged APIs 76
Web APIs, certified APIs
bluetooth API 81
camera API 81
Idle API 81
mobile connection 81
network stats API 81
permission API 82
power management API 81
settings API 81
telephony 81
time/clock API 82
WebSMS 81
web application
converting, to hosted Firefox OS
  application 128-130
WebIDE
developer tools, using 18
installing 11-14
used, for creating new apps 14-17
used, for installing new apps 14-17
wifi 77

X

XAMPP
URL 37

Thank you for buying
Learning Firefox OS Application Development

About Packt Publishing

Packt, pronounced 'packed', published its first book, *Mastering phpMyAdmin for Effective MySQL Management*, in April 2004, and subsequently continued to specialize in publishing highly focused books on specific technologies and solutions.

Our books and publications share the experiences of your fellow IT professionals in adapting and customizing today's systems, applications, and frameworks. Our solution-based books give you the knowledge and power to customize the software and technologies you're using to get the job done. Packt books are more specific and less general than the IT books you have seen in the past. Our unique business model allows us to bring you more focused information, giving you more of what you need to know, and less of what you don't.

Packt is a modern yet unique publishing company that focuses on producing quality, cutting-edge books for communities of developers, administrators, and newbies alike. For more information, please visit our website at www.packtpub.com.

About Packt Open Source

In 2010, Packt launched two new brands, Packt Open Source and Packt Enterprise, in order to continue its focus on specialization. This book is part of the Packt Open Source brand, home to books published on software built around open source licenses, and offering information to anybody from advanced developers to budding web designers. The Open Source brand also runs Packt's Open Source Royalty Scheme, by which Packt gives a royalty to each open source project about whose software a book is sold.

Writing for Packt

We welcome all inquiries from people who are interested in authoring. Book proposals should be sent to author@packtpub.com. If your book idea is still at an early stage and you would like to discuss it first before writing a formal book proposal, then please contact us; one of our commissioning editors will get in touch with you.

We're not just looking for published authors; if you have strong technical skills but no writing experience, our experienced editors can help you develop a writing career, or simply get some additional reward for your expertise.

Learning Ionic

ISBN: 978-1-78355-260-3 Paperback: 388 pages

Build real-time and hybrid mobile applications with Ionic

1. Create hybrid mobile applications by combining the capabilities of Ionic, Cordova, and AngularJS.

2. Reduce the time to market your application using Ionic, that helps in rapid application development.

3. Detailed code examples and explanations, helping you get up and running with Ionic quickly and easily.

Mastering OpenCV Android Application Programming

ISBN: 978-1-78398-820-4 Paperback: 216 pages

Master the art of implementing computer vision algorithms on Android platforms to build robust and efficient applications

1. Understand and utilise the features of OpenCV, Android SDK, and OpenGL.

2. Detect and track specific objects in a video using Optical Flow and Lucas Kanade Tracker.

3. An advanced guide full of real-world examples, helping you to build smart OpenCV Android applications.

Please check **www.PacktPub.com** for information on our titles

Mastering Julia

ISBN: 978-1-78355-331-0   Paperback: 410 pages

Develop your analytical and programming skills further in Julia to solve complex data processing problems

1. Build statistical models with linear regression and analysis of variance (ANOVA).

2. Author your own modules and contribute information to the Julia package system.

3. Engage yourself in a data science project through the entire cycle of ETL, analytics, and data visualization.

Android 5 Programming by Example

ISBN: 9781-7-8528-844-9   Paperback: 212 pages

Turn your ideas into elegant and powerful mobile applications using the latest Android Studio for the Android Lollipop platform

1. Design and customize GUI using material design to create attractive and intuitive layouts easily.

2. Bring your designs to life with Android 5's powerful and extensive Java libraries, new sensors, and new platforms such as TVs, wearables, and cars.

3. An example-based guide to learn and develop applications for Android 5.

Please check **www.PacktPub.com** for information on our titles

www.ingramcontent.com/pod-product-compliance
Lightning Source LLC
Chambersburg PA
CBHW060141060326
40690CB00018B/3934